DIRECTING CREATIVITY

THE ART OF INNOVATION

ALAN WILLIAMS

Silverscreen Consulting
Innovative Solutions

Published in the United States of America by Silverscreen Consulting. *www.silverscreenconsulting.com*

First Edition

ISBN: 978-0-9863225-6-3

ISBN: 978-0-9863225-7-0 (soft cover)

ISBN: 978-0-9863225-8-7 (eBook)

Cover design by Thomas Leavitt

❖ ENDORSEMENTS

"Write the book on Creativity and keep adding value to others!"

~ John C. Maxwell, New York Times best-selling author and leadership expert

"The short film, *WHY MAN CREATES, changed my life. Since then, I've been immersed in creativity and astonished by the clearly mystical process. Of the unbounded expressions of creativity, music is the quintessential manifestation. In Directing Creativity: The Art of Innovation, *Alan has managed to demystify the process in practical, accessible terms that are applicable to every innovative passion."* (*Why Man Creates. Saul Bass, Academy Award, 1968)

~ Kieth Merrill, Academy Award winning producer, director, screenwriter and author

"Using his experience as a film composer, Alan Williams articulates simply and beautifully the mysterious process of creation, and in doing so argues convincingly that anyone and everyone can create by committing fearlessly to a few simple

steps. A wise and encouraging look at one of the great mysteries of human consciousness."

~ Sterling Van Wagenen, Co-founder, The Sundance Film Festival, and award winning film producer

"To have innovation, you have to be creative. This book shows how to start with a blank page and fill it with success."

~ Jeffrey Hayzlett, Chairman & CEO, C-Suite Network, TV & Radio Host, Speaker, Author and Part-Time Cowboy

"Executing your vision is never done alone and the creative process can be much stronger when developed in a team. Directing Creativity empowers others to share in that creative vision, which by doing so makes any outcome even better."

~ Shep Hyken, CSP, CPAE, New York Times and Wall Street Journal Bestselling author, Chief Amazement Officer of Shepard Presentations

"Directing Creativity demystifies the creative process. If you seek to take your creative strategies and perspective to the next level, this book contains the clear process and inspiration you are looking for."

~ Mark Sanborn CSP, CPAE, New York Times and Wall Street Journal Bestselling Author of The Fred Factor and The Potential Principle, President of Sanborn and Associates, Inc.

"Many of us are creative thinkers and can get lost in executing our creative ideas. Alan Williams' groundbreaking book Directing Creativity *is the blueprint required to harness our creative powers into the actionable steps that stakeholders and team members alike can understand, contribute to, and act upon."*

~ Suzanne Meldeau Leonard, Founder and CEO Legends and Legacy, Inc., Former Executive Director at The Speed of Trust Practice with Stephen M. R. Covey

"Composer Alan Williams shows you how to take your creative ideas and make them reality through a step-by-step process that expands the original idea, growing it to its full potential. Directing Creativity *is useful for people in any creative field, and for those looking to get there."*

~ Alan Rast, VP Special Ops, FOX Television

"We must adapt and adjust to an ever-evolving, ever changing global business climate. Directing Creativity *empowers your*

organization to drive innovation as a core competency and to communicate it effectively across all levels and functions of the entity."

~ Daniel J Gilmartin, Former CFO at Meeting Professionals International, Former President and COO at Frank's Nursery and Crafts, COO at American Blind and Wallpaper Factory

"Within each member of your teams is latent creative genius. Further, all have a fundamental desire to be their best selves and to bring their best to the workplace. You can effectively unleash this magnificent force through Directing Creativity. *A powerful 5-step proven process will transform results within any organization who applies it."*

~ Dale R. Bond, former VP at Medquest Pharmacy, former Senior Client Partner at FranklinCovey Co., former President at D.R. Bond & Associates, former EVP/COO at Ameriseal

"Directing Creativity *is simply amazing! Our Executive Team uses Alan Williams' Innovation Process to unleash their creative energy and chart our future."*

~ Steven Spiker, Executive Vice President Entertainment Partners

"If you've ever struggled turning creativity into a consistent reality, then Alan Williams' insightful masterpiece, Directing Creativity, *is your guide. This insightful book delivers not only the principles for your creative journey but will inspire the hope and energy needed to truly make your ideas soar!"*

> ~ Dr. Matt Townsend, Founder of Townsend Relationship Center, TV and Radio Host, Author and former lead presenter, Franklin Covey

"The workplace is changing every day with emerging technologies and industries. Delivering education that is relevant requires innovative thinking and strategic planning. Alan Williams' Directing Creativity *offers solutions to channel creativity into ideas that can be implemented within any organization."*

> ~ Dr. Diane Van Hook, Chancellor, Santa Clarita Community College District

"Music binds the soul of people. Alan Williams as a composer captures the heart. But by sharing his knowledge, his own experiences, Alan is now opening up the path for others to capture their own, bring out the best of themselves and that of others. Anyone around the world can us the steps of Directing Creativity *to form richer innovations and it's cyclical. The*

more you apply these steps to enhance outcomes, the more you will naturally succeed."

~ Dilma Arends Geerman, Director at Neca INK, In-
vestigative Reporter at Aruba Awe, Chairperson at
Foundacion Austims Aruba, Former Contributor at
The Economist

CONTENTS

ACKNOWLEDGEMENTS

No real creative success is achieved alone. This has proved especially true while writing this book. There are countless individuals who have directly and indirectly inspired me along the pathway of writing the book DIRECTING CREATIVITY.

Thank you Greg Gardner for planting the seed. Thank you John C. Maxwell for encouraging me to share my creative process. Thank you Patrick West, Dale Bond, Matt Townsend, Lynn Gardner and Randall Jones for your insight and advice. Thank you Thomas Leavitt for your beautiful, original cover art. Thank you to the many global organizations that allowed me to share and validate the concepts of this book, especially those of you in the far corners of the world who proved that the Innovation Process works everywhere.

Thank you Suzanne Meldeau Leonard for sharing this journey with me, for tirelessly urging me on to do my best work, for helping me to discover just the right word and phrase and for being a true super-champion.

Thank you to my piano and composition teachers during my formative years for instilling in me the quest for excellence and for helping me begin to identity my own creative process.

Thank you mom and dad for letting me dream big and for always cheering me on in the seemingly impossible. Thank you Brandon, Connor and Devin for always being encouraging sons. Finally a special thank you Julianne for endless support, our partnership together in life, and for so very much more.

---❖---

FORWARD

The prospect of talking to Alan Williams scared me to death.

Yes, I'm a firm believer in Alan's assessment that "everyone is creative." True, I make my living in celebration of creative thinkers. What's more, I am musically inclined, so terms like key signature, quarter note and forte don't intimidate me.

However, Alan's ingenuity manifests itself in a way I find incomprehensible: He writes film scores — a skill that is certainly NOT my forte.

Was I about to look really stupid?

But wait, I've SEEN movies, haven't I? Thanks to composer Max Steiner, I get goosebumps during the orchestrally enriched opening of *Gone with the Wind*. I figuratively run for dry land when I hear John Williams' theme from *Jaws*. And Mike Oldfield's Tubular Bells from *The Exorcist* almost landed 11-year-old me in therapy.

Most of us have heard music described as "the universal language." DIRECTING CREATVITY is a *thought-full* exploration of this indisputable truth. Anywhere you go in the world, a G-sharp is going to be a G-sharp and "accelerando"— a gradual increase in tempo — is going to put a little extra spring in a musician's step.

But emotionally speaking, human beings are universally moved by sound. And just as we collectively house myriad unborn creative thoughts, we have an innate connection to a variety of styles of music.

Alan simply asserts that, regardless of your profession, "a blank piece of paper is a blank piece of paper." We are all confronted with this often career-threatening hurdle — when the next BIG IDEA simply won't come. In DIRECTING CREATIVITY, Alan Williams brilliantly illustrates the steps involved in *filling in the blank.* Although the connective tissue is music composition, the connective issue is the unlocking of your imagination.

Through the systematic, provocative breakdown of his personal creative process, Alan beautifully demystifies what it means to be "creative." And as creativity is the cornerstone of innovation, you don't need a PhD in Music Composition to understand that following a proven process is instrumental *(yep, I did that on purpose!)* to ongoing success.

Did I have a reason to be fearful of Alan Williams? No. Will readers of DIRECTING CREATIVITY be able to compose a symphony? Probably not. But everyone, *everywhere* has the need — the instinct — to create SOMETHING. And pretty much everybody understands the joy, the heart-pumping anticipation that occurs when you're about to embark upon a journey and *follow the yellow brick road.*

Look at it this way, give almost any child a blank piece of paper and a box of crayons and he or she will create a masterpiece. DIRECTING CREATIVITY is Alan Williams' brilliant guide to his wizardry, and to rediscovering your perpetually inspired inner child. So grab your box of intellectual crayons and let's get going.

Randall Kenneth Jones

Author, SHOW ME: Celebrities, Business Tycoons, Rock Stars, Journalists, Humanitarians, Attack Bunnies & More!

INTRODUCTION

The lights dim in the theater. The curtains slowly part, unveiling a dark, blank movie screen. There is a rising expectation to be swept away on a distant expedition, far away from day-to-day life. The anticipation is palpable and swells throughout the room.

As the curtains reach their resting place, lights slowly emerge on the screen. Images begin to appear and sounds fill the space enveloping the senses ... the journey begins. The music crescendos and we are swept away. A movie is born.

I am a composer. I write music for these films. My contribution to the film is to heighten each viewer's senses along the story's path. My job? Breathe emotional life into the characters and enhance the audience's connection to the story through a musical score. The 2-dimensional images projected on the silver screen rely on my music to manifest the drama within the hearts and minds of the audience.

The music I create helps the audience feel a myriad of emotions. From anguishing fear to celebratory joy, and from the angst of tragedy to the jubilation of true love, I have learned how to underscore every human emotion with music.

Where does the music come from? How does it become a musical score in a film?

The same questions could be asked of the film itself: Where did the images come from? How did the characters come to be? How did this movie become a movie? How does any idea become a reality?

For a motion picture and for any form of creation or innovation:

Creativity is the catalyst!

There are many who talk about innovation and creativity. Many books have been written about famous individuals addressing their incredible contribution by way of creativity and innovation. These works are primarily written through the authors' lens. They provide observations and commentaries about famous figures that have made significant impacts on our lives and the world. Others address creativity through scientific observations of brain function. While these supply insight to creative individuals and illuminate the science behind it, they typically don't offer a hands-on, step-by-step approach to the actual creative process.

Unlike a historian or scientist, I am uniquely qualified to address this subject. After all, I use my creativity in life and in the studio to solve dramatic problems every day! Yes, life often imitates art and I apply these problem-solving skills to both.

My own creative process hadn't occurred to me until one day a friend who ran a global enterprise, with employees working in over 120 countries, asked me to come and talk to his senior management. His request was both simple and profound, "I don't get how you take a blank piece of paper and create music. And you know that our company is striving to become more innovative in the solutions we offer. Is there any chance you would come and talk to us about what you do as a film composer? Can you help us become more creative?"

After the word "sure" was out of my mouth, I realized that I'd never taken a close look at my own creative process. How did I turn a blank page into notes that emotionally bonded a film to an audience? I thank my friend often for posing that question to me, as it prompted my own discovery about the creative process.

So, how DO I write music?

I have degrees from top universities where I learned theory, harmony, counterpoint and orchestration. Yet much of what I do is simply intuitive, and instinctive. I respond emotionally to a film, its story and characters, and translate those emotions into music. How can I teach this to people in a corporate environment, culturally diverse, controlled, and most often believe they are non-creative?

Out of necessity, I found myself looking at my own creative process and breaking down the basic components of what I do as a composer. Delving even deeper into the process, I discovered steps that I follow on every project. In composing there were basic steps, an algorithm that I always followed. I actually have a structured creative process that filled the blank pages with musical notes!

Given this application of my thoughts on creativity, I quickly discovered that these steps do not just apply to composing music. They provide a framework for *all* creativity and innovation. The steps I use to create music are the same steps that all innovators use, whether they realize it or not.

For most creators and innovators, like myself, these steps have become intuitive. This leads to the purpose for this book ...

Unveil the steps innovators use to create.

Creativity is simply the mental process of generating new ideas or concepts. Any idea, process, solution, invention or product IS the result of creativity. You don't have to be an artist, composer, movie director or inventor to create and innovate – we all are creative!

Creativity often seems like a daunting prospect, especially to those individuals who believe they are not "creative". Only after working with my friend's company, and subsequently with many others around the world, have I discovered that we all have the potential to feed and grow our individual creativity. We ALL can foster new ideas and create new innovations and opportunities.

As a motion picture, television and documentary film composer, I have spent 25 years working in Hollywood writing musical scores to over 100 projects. Although each film was different in subject matter and musical approach, my creative process has remained the same. In fact, I used this exact same process to write this book. It is a process that has illuminated my own path of discovery, as I applied these critical steps of creation. Once mastered, you too will discover that there are new, exciting and limitless prospects of potential within you waiting to be freed.

Since the first time I was asked to share my creative process with those executives in Los Angeles, I have traveled around the globe teaching these steps in the innovation process with individuals across all levels and functions of global business, the public sector, in communities, throughout educational systems, as well as a range of other organizations. It has, at times, been breathtaking to see these steps apply cross-culturally and generationally, bridging all sorts of socio-economic gaps and helping highly diverse groups learn how to become innovators.

At one of these events where I shared this message, I spent time with John Maxwell, a titan in the non-fiction publishing and speaking industries. While together in Aruba, during our speaking tour of the Caribbean, John and I talked about my presentation on creativity. At some point I mentioned to John that I was thinking about writing a book about the subject. A few weeks after returning home John sent me a personal note in the mail that simply read, "Write the book on Creativity and keep adding value to others!"

So I have.

Steve Jobs famously said, "Creativity is just having enough dots to connect."

This book will help guide you through the creative process as you learn the key steps of innovation – discovering enough dots to connect. This book will systematically move you from idea to creation, from concept to product, from your deepest dreams to your magnificent reality!

Now I ask, "How important is innovation to you?"

Maybe you are the rare exception and are perfectly content with everything around you, with your life and in your profession. If, like the rest of us, you see there is room for improvement, then consider this book a creative upgrade as you uncover how to direct your creativity, and provide innovative contributions into your life, family, company and world.

Consider this, the Stone Age didn't end because they ran out of stones. It ended because of innovation. Innovation fostered this change and was driven by creativity.

Whatever your profession, position or passion, as you begin *Directing Creativity* you will discover that you too are an artist of innovation. Once you embark on this journey, applying the steps of innovation, the results will be numerous. The solutions to problems become plentiful and your dreams become YOUR treasured creations!

CHAPTER 1

✦

PITCH BLACK

The Blank Page

C reativity always begins in darkness. It can be an all-consuming darkness if you are not prepared to confront it and direct it. Creativity requires seeding, cultivating and nurturing. It is in the preparation to direct your creativity where true innovation begins.

Every musical score I write begins the same way, with a blank page. For every writer there is a blank page. For artists, it's a blank canvas, for sculptors a block of marble and for the inventor, the unknown, undiscovered idea.

Preparation seems like the natural beginning for most tasks. The same is true for creativity. A runner wouldn't think of getting up one day and going out to run a marathon. Training is essential preparation for the 26.2 mile run. It begins with short runs followed by longer training sessions to prepare a runner for the grueling race. Only when stamina and strength increase can a runner consider a marathon. It would be crazy to simply start running without this preparation in hopes to finish the race.

Preparing for creativity is no different. Even with my 25 years of experience, I can't simply sit down and begin composing a score. Nor can you expect to sit down and suddenly flip a switch and have free-flowing inspiration. Creativity requires the right climate, an environment consisting of the necessary tools and proper conditions to produce creative fruit.

Before I pick up my pencil to begin composing, my mind must be clear and ready to tap into my creativity. Before any creative action is taken, I must be free from distractions. These distractions can manifest themselves in many different forms; there are the mental distractions, physical distractions, and even emotional distractions that stand in the way of unabated creativity.

The studio is my creative sanctuary. It is, by design, a safe place to open up my emotions and invite in ideas, both musically and with any other creative endeavor I'm pursuing. The studio is free from physical clutter and the writing desk is clean and organized. After all, I can't expect my mind to be free to create if my physical surroundings are cluttered and unorganized.

Looking around my studio, I see objects that bring me peace, joy and encouragement. Awards remind me that I can successfully create musical scores. Objects from my travels instill confidence in my ideas. A large window to the outside world provides natural light, as well as the unlimited possibilities the world beyond my studio has to offer.

Then there are my tools; my piano, my computers and all of the electronic equipment found in most recording studios. These tools give me the ability to compose the musical scores. Without these tools how can I be expected to create and produce anything? How could I possibly compose that next masterpiece?

Finally, as I look around my studio, I notice maybe the most important element – silence. Quiet, noiseless silence is one of the most crucial elements in my creative space. I can't compose with the phone ringing, conversations taking place around me, or other disruptive distractions. Neither can you. I must block out the noise of the world; emails, phone calls, and every other interruption needs to be eliminated from our creative spaces and frame of mind if we want to tap into our creative potential.

Thomas Edison said, "The best thinking has been done in solitude. The worst has been done in turmoil." Quiet solitude is the fertile soil where seeds of creation take root.

Once the environment is prepared, it's time to return to the blank page. The page itself can be daunting, just as the prospect of creating can be. However, the process of creating is exciting, albeit also terrifying.

When I begin a project I often ask myself, "What new score can I write that I haven't already written? How will I ever compose 75 minutes of music for a 100-piece orchestra in only 4 weeks? What if I can't come up with any good musical ideas? Will the audience like my music? Will the director like what I write? Will I be satisfied or even like what I compose?"

I find that my mind wants to doubt its creative potential before I even begin composing and I've learned from other creative professionals in my industry that I am not alone. I'm going to share a little Hollywood-insider information; this occurs on nearly every project. One would think that after these 25 years of experience composing film scores, this doubt would go away. It doesn't. Doubt always finds a way to creep into the creative process. No matter what past success I have enjoyed, nor previous experience gleaned, doubt still rears its ugly head.

The only way to remove doubt is through action.

I'm often asked, "What do you do when you get 'writer's block'?" My answer has always been the same, "Firm deadlines prevent writer's block!" In other words, I can't miss the deadline leading up to a recording session. The movie has a release date and the music is always the last element added to the film before it is released to the public.

Before I begin composing, I am clear on what my deadline is and use this deadline as a catalyst for my creativity. It gives me the supportive urgency and challenge to create-on-demand. So even though doubt tries to derail my creative process right from the get-go, I have a firm deadline to deliver the musical score.

In the summer of 1997, I received a phone call from the Academy Award-winning director, Kieth Merrill. He wanted to know if I might be available to write the score for his IMAX film, *Amazon*. For me, this was a long-awaited phone call that could elevate my career as a composer to a new level. This would be a wide-release film requiring a large orchestral score to be written and produced.

I could not get the words out quick enough, "Absolutely I'm interested." Then there was the dreaded follow-up question, "So Kieth, when do you need the score completed by?" There was a short pause on the other end of the phone and Kieth reluctantly replied, "The final mix of the film is in 2 weeks. Can you get on a plane in the morning and fly to meet me in Northern California to preview the film?"

That very next day I was sitting with the famed Oscar-winning director talking about the music I would compose to fill the IMAX theaters, which are the size of an eight-story building with screens that are wider than they are tall! The music must be equally as powerful and would require a large Hollywood orchestra complete with ethnic woodwinds, percussion players and a choir. The reality began to sink in, I had only 13 days to write, record and mix the 40 minutes of music for the film. That meant only about 7 days of actual composing time.

With this eminent deadline looming over me, and knowing that action diminishes my doubt, there was one hurdle that remained in my way. For many of us, the greatest hurdle to overcome in the creative process is that nasty four-letter word that squelches most people in their creative endeavors: FEAR.

Fear is a powerful form of thought and has the power to paralyze our physical and mental nerve centers. Fear always exists each time I begin a new project. When I've talked about his with other composers, writers and artist, they all express that the same sentiment exists for them – a fear of failure. Fear and doubt share the same mind-debilitating space and affects our creative potential.

Fear cannot coexist with creation.

The two conflicting and competing attitudes cannot co-habitate in a creative-seeking individual's mind. T.S. Eliot has said, "Anxiety is the hand maiden of creativity."

Of course, we all want to succeed and we never set out to fail. With creativity however, we all fail. In fact we will fail, fail, and fail again. We will fail until we ultimately succeed. We must get over our anxiety of failure because the fear of making a mistake will halt our creative energy. It's only when you realize that every idea you have won't be fantastic, you are then free to come up with a overabundance of ideas, even some bad ideas and yes, ideas that will eventually fail.

With pencil in hand, I look at my blank page. It is clear that I don't have the luxury to allow my fear to take hold. I must be creative on-demand. Starting now and missing the deadline for this tremendous opportunity is not an option.

I spent seven intensity-filled days creating the epic score for *Amazon*. It was my first large-scale orchestral score, recorded by the finest musicians in the world. I conducted the team of world-class musicians at the famed Sony Pictures Scoring Stage in Los Angeles. The magnitude of the project gave way to many forms of fear, but I had to overcome them and perform, which I did.

Amazon went on to receive an Academy Award nomination in 1998 for *Best Documentary Short Film* and launched my career in the IMAX film world. To date, *Amazon* remains one of the most fulfilling creative experiences I have had. The score still stands as my professional creative standard of success and is a reminder that overcoming fear is all in a days work.

I love the example of the advertising company Grey New York. They give out a "Heroic Failure" trophy once each quarter to the person who takes a big, edgy risk and fails, even if the idea had clearly seemed like a good idea in the beginning.

Then there is SurePayroll, a company in Glenview, Illinois who intentionally create a culture where its team members can remove their fear of failure. To accomplish this, the CEO created an award called "Best New Mistake". Only the people who are trying to do a good job will make mistakes and learn from them. Only these team members are eligible for the company's $400 annual cash award.

Most companies don't want to fail, or admit to failure, yet their cautious and paralyzing practices ultimately leads them right into failure. Liberating an organization and its individuals from the fear of failure will go a long way to fostering creativity, innovation and ultimately, success.

Failure is not all bad.

You must fail to become innovative! Let's consider the maverick filmmaker Woody Allen. He certainly doesn't let failure get in the way of his creative process, "If you're not failing every now and again, it's a sign you're not doing anything very innovative."

The very fact that every note I write in a new musical score does not make it in the final film frees my mind to create. I accept that every melody I compose isn't worthy of an award and that all of my musical themes are not destined to be memorable. Any scene of a movie, however, can and often does have numerous variations to the musical approach until the perfect solution is finally realized. In other words, I compose hours and hours of music that will never make it into a movie. I write music that you will never hear and fail as a composer long before I succeed as a composer.

Knowing that you will fail helps to remove the fear of failing.

When I tell myself that all ideas are not created equal and that most of my musical ideas will not be brilliant, something wonderful happens. I give my mind permission to freely consider all my creative ideas – the bad ones, the misguided ones, the obvious ones and even the most outrageous ones. I liberate my creativity because I remove the restraints of fear. I consciously tell myself, "Failing is OK!" I know I'm going to do it so I might as well get over it! Giving way to this path of thinking frees up our creativity.

Thomas Edison famously said, "I failed my way to success." You never know where those failures will take you. For Thomas Edison, failure never got in the way of his ability to innovate. "I make more mistakes than anyone else I know, and sooner or later, I patent most of them!"

I love Tina Turner's philosophy. "Sometimes you've got to let everything go – purge yourself. If you are unhappy with anything, whatever is bringing you down, get rid of it. Because you'll find that when you're free, your true creativity, your true self comes out."

The lesson? Purge yourself of all self-doubt and especially purge yourself of fear.

There is a mental debate that takes place within us all, and frankly it need not exist at all despite the fact we all fear failure. Liberating our creativity with the knowledge that we all will fail on our road to innovation somehow turns the self-conscious mind into a self-believing force.

Changing your internal dialog will transform you into that self-believing force! I am creative. I can generate new ideas and concepts. I have the power to innovate.

This positive and honest thinking allows me to look at the blank page as a medium for endless possibilities to be born. The blank page no longer represents fear and failure, rather it holds undiscovered treasures and wonderment yet to be made manifest.

There is a game I like to play while composing a film score. What will be the most surprising revelation that will come out of this process? Will it be a memorable theme? Will it be the perfect dramatic solution for that one challenging scene? Or will it be some new musical sound that I have yet to discover?

I can honestly say that for every score I have written, there has always been this revealing moment during the process. It's like unwrapping a gift and discovering that inside is something far better than ever hoped for.

The sense of discovery when unwrapping that gift is invigorating and fantastic. You never know what you will uncover as you begin the creative process. I do know that when I look back after completing a score, the page is no longer blank but filled in with just the right combination of notes to give the audience that perfect emotional experience. I can vividly see those musical and dramatic discoveries come to life, and marvel each time I complete a movie score or at the creation of a new musical piece. I have created something new and given birth to my ideas that are now available for the world to experience.

Creativity is exciting and addictive.

The more I create, the more I want to create. Interestingly enough, the more I create, the easier it is to create.

Like a well-conditioned runner, my creativity has more stamina as it races one marathon after another.

Don't fear the blank page. Embrace it. We all begin with one. Savor the journey that is about to begin, as creativity, inspiration and innovation are about to take flight!

CHAPTER 2

❖

ONCE UPON A TIME

The Art of Possibility

Creativity and innovation begin with the art of possibility.

We all have an incredible capacity to produce thoughts and ideas. We have the unlimited power to compose, conceive and construct possibilities. In these creations, in fact with all creations, we must first begin with our imagination.

Henry David Thoreau said, "The world is but a canvas to the imagination."

Imagination is our power to create in one's mind.

Step 1 - *Imagine*

Imagination is the spark that ignites our creativity. It is our ability to form mental images, sensations and concepts, long before they exist in reality. Imagination provides a way to visualize and experience anything our mind can conceive.

I'm reminded of a story told of two men, both seriously ill, who occupied the same hospital room. One man was allowed to sit up in his bed for an hour each afternoon to help drain the fluid from his lungs. His bed was next to the room's only window, while the other man had to spend all his time flat on his back. The men would talk for hours on end. They spoke of their wives and families, their homes, their jobs, their time in the military and where they had been on vacation.

Every afternoon when the man in the bed by the window could sit up, he would pass the time by describing to his roommate all the things he could see outside the window. The man in the other bed began to live for those one-hour periods where his world would be broadened and enlivened by all the activity and color of the world outside.

The window overlooked a park with a lovely lake where ducks and swans played on the water, while children sailed their model boats. Young lovers strolled arm in arm amidst flowers bursting of color and a fine view of the city's skyline could be seen in the distance. As the man by the window described all this in exquisite detail, the man on the other side of the room would lay with his eyes closed imagining the picturesque scene.

One sunny afternoon the man by the window described the parade passing by on the street below. Although the man on the other side couldn't hear the band, his imagination could see it clearly as the old fellow by the window described its every detail with the most vivid words.

The days and weeks passed, as the highly anticipated afternoon peeks into the outside world continued. There were bright, sunny days, and rainy days too. Dark clouds would roll in, while intense lightning bolts descended upon the park. Pedestrians would run for cover as the rain came down in sheets and swirled around the streets blown by the howling wind. "Soon it would be winter," one said and speculated if the pond would freeze hard enough for skaters. "I wonder if there be a Christmas tree on the frozen lake this year and carolers too?" the other added. They wondered about how much snow they might get this year.

One morning, the nurse arrived to bring water for their baths to find the lifeless body of the man by the window, who had died peacefully in his sleep. She was saddened and quickly called the hospital attendants to take the body away.

Not long after, the other man asked if he could be moved next to the window. The nurse was happy to make the switch and after being assured that he was comfortable, she left him alone.

Slowly, painfully, he propped himself up on one elbow to take his first look at the real world outside. He strained to slowly turn and look out the window beside the bed. To his surprise ... it faced a completely blank brick wall.

It was Albert Einstein who proclaimed, "Imagination is everything. It is the preview of life's coming attractions." He also admitted, "When I examine myself and my methods of thought, I come to the conclusion that the gift of fantasy has meant more to me than my talent for absorbing positive knowledge."

The power of our imagination is undeniable. The great 19th century English poet and painter William Blake believed, "What is now proved was once only imagined." Going a step further, there is a Japanese proverb that says, "There is nothing that cannot be achieved by firm imagination."

Imagination is not simply daydreaming.
Imagination is power.

Successful leaders, businesses and organizations know the power of imagination. Bill Gates, the founder of Microsoft, said that his company "is a company that manages imagination." These leaders know how to ignite and harness this power of imagination in their own lives as well as in the lives of those in their organizations.

When Apple's Steve Jobs joined Disney's corporate board after he acquired Pixar in 2006, his advice to Disney was, "Dream Bigger!" This was in response to Disney's plans to turn its retail stores into miniature interactive theme parks. Following this advice, Disney pumped around $340 million into a complete refit of its stores and rebranded them as 'Imagination Parks'.

In four short years since the rebrand of its stores, the Imagination Parks in the United Kingdom alone made $761.6 million in revenue with total revenue of $1.3 billion from their 348 stores worldwide. Disney's Imagination Parks now account for 15% of the entire company's annual revenue.

Imagination is the first step in directing creativity. Using our imagination is a skill that all too often has been overlooked, abandoned and even discouraged.

The best kept secret to exercising our imagination in the innovation process can be found in one simple word: *Remember*

Childhood oozes with enthusiasm and fantasy. Children use their imaginations every day. It does not matter where they grew up, what their cultural background is or even their family's economic conditions. All children use their imagination.

Remember what it was like when you were five and you believed that you could do anything? Your imagination had no limits. What children don't know or what they have not experienced erases all limiting thoughts, fear and doubt. They don't know when something *appears* to be impossible therefore everything *is* possible.

Let's do a quick exercise in remembering:

- What were some of the things you imagined as a child?

- What did you believe you could do?

- Did you believe that you were a magical princess or maybe a superhero with special powers?

- Did you believe that you could fly?

- What did you imagine you would be when you grew up?

I remember as a child playing for hours outside with friends. We would act out the greatest battles, travel to other planets and participate in secret spy missions. We executed all of these epic events by simply using our imagination. If we needed special weapons, instruments or spy gadgets, there were plenty of sticks and other objects we found in the garage. These became the tools we needed to achieve our objectives.

If some of our friends doubted our ability to perform any seemingly impossible feat, we simply disregarded them and sought out new friends that would not dampen our enthusiasm. Everything was possible. We knew it and we believed it!

If you take a few minutes to reflect on your childhood, can you remember the magic that existed in your imagination?

"Every child is an artist. The problem is how to remain an artist once he grows up." The great artist Pablo Picasso recognized that too many of us have grown up and forgotten how to use our imagination.

As we take time to *remember* how we used this imagination as children, we will *remember* and recognize its power within us. Now we can use that same skill to unlock our creativity.

In early stages of learning, educators understand this power as we are taught to use our imagination. Teachers read stories aloud as we visualize in our mind the images from these stories. In our mind we could see the characters and their surroundings clearly. The stories of fantasy, mystery and adventure would unfold in perfect detail through our imagination. It's no wonder that bedtime stories are so popular amongst children.

Many of our early school assignments would be to sketch and color what we imagined a story would look like. This exercise was not to determine how good an artist we were, but to help us translate our thoughts into reality through our drawings. Taking an abstract thought and making it real on paper was simply transforming our imagination into reality.

As we grew older, our school experiences began to change us. We were taught the importance of facts. We memorized terms and equations, theories and methods. With each passing year, we filled our minds with more and more 'knowledge' and less and less 'creative imagination'. It is no wonder that as adults our ability to imagine has become a bit rusty as a skill.

Albert Einstein said it best, "It is a miracle that curiosity survives formal education." He went on to say, "Imagination is more important than knowledge. For while knowledge defines all we currently know and understand, imagination points to all we might yet discover and create."

Remembering our inner-child requires forgetting what we believe is and is not possible and instead believing that everything IS possible. We all have the ability to retain that child within us. Do you remember how?

The great author Ernest Hemingway believed, "The thing is to become a master and in your old age to acquire the courage to do what children did when they knew nothing."

Walt Disney knew the power of his imagination. For Walt, dreaming had no limits. On many occasions he said, "If you can dream it, you can do it." He created Mickey Mouse in 1928 as the world's first fully–synchronized sound cartoon. His imagination continued to flourish as he created the first full-length animated musical feature, "Snow White and the Seven Dwarfs."

Walt Disney's grand masterpiece of vision and imagination was his creation of Disneyland. Walt imagined building a tourist attraction to entertain fans of his movies. Since the theme park opened in 1955, more than 2 billion people have been entertained, including celebrities, presidents, kings and queens from all over the globe. Disneyland began as an idea, imagined by a master-dreamer, and now stands as Walt's greatest creation.

Today, the Walt Disney Company has an entire division dedicated to design and development. It's called Walt

Disney Imagineering. Its sole purpose is the creation and construction of Disney theme parks, resorts, cruise ships and entertainment venues worldwide.

Disney Imagineers have few restrictions when developing new concepts. When improving upon existing attractions, the Imagineers return to the creative child within – where some of the most brilliant solutions emerge as solutions to complex problems.

The popular attraction "Soarin' Over California" is one example. The Imagineeers knew they wanted guests to experience the sensation of flight, but weren't sure how to accomplish the task of loading people on to a ride in an efficient manner where everyone had an optimal viewing position. One day, an Imagineer found an Erector set in his attic and with this old childhood toy, he was able to envision and design a ride vehicle that would effectively simulate hang gliding.

Now you might say, "I'm not a very imaginative person" or "I'm no Walt Disney". Isn't it clear that the power to imagine is within us all? And as you practice this skill of igniting your own imagination, your mind will open up to discover the incredible potential of your creativity.

This process of seeing within your imagination is known as *visualizing* or creating a mental picture. Visualization is a tool we use in the imagination process.

Walt Disney visualized Disneyland in his mind before it became one of the most-visited tourist attractions in the world. You too must visualize the results before you begin the act of creation, as any expected change or desired result always begins with "seeing" those results first.

Directing your creativity requires seeing the end in your mind *before* you begin.

In Italy during the 16th century, Pope Leo X commissioned many great works of art from the best creative artists of the time. They included the greats like Rafael and Michelangelo. Giorgio Vasari, a painter, architect and writer, often called "the first art historian", chronicled many of these great artists of the day. Vasari's work, *The Lives of the Most Excellent Painters, Sculptors, and Architects* detailed an account of Leonardo da Vinci and his patron, Pope Leo. Upon being given a commission from Pope Leo X, da Vinci immediately went to work to distil oils and herbs, in order to make the varnish; at which point Pope Leo said,

"Alas! This man will never do anything, for he begins by thinking of the end of the work, before the beginning."

Leonardo da Vinci understood visualizing the end of his work before he ever picked up a brush, chisel or pencil. Da Vinci's creativity always began first with his imagination.

The power of imagination is also well defined by Charles F. Haanel in his book *The Master Key System*, "Imagination is the light by which we can penetrate new worlds of thought and experience. Imagination is the mighty instrument by which every discoverer, every inventor, opened the way from precedent to experience. Precedent said, 'It cannot be done,' experience said, 'It is done.' Imagination is the constructive form of thought which must precede every constructive action. A builder cannot build a structure of any kind until he has first received the plans from the architect, and the architect must get them from his imagination."

In *Cracking Creativity*, Michael Michalko describes how a group of Department of Defense weapons specialists were faced with the challenge of modifying missiles. They were stumped. Finally, one of the participants suggested that the group take an imaginary excursion into the desert. For ten minutes, the engineers and scientists imagined walking through a desert and listed everything they saw and experienced. One of the participants imagined seeing a "sidewinder," a poisonous snake, while someone else remarked that a sidewinder locates its prey by sensing body heat. This inspired the idea of an air-to-air missile that homes in on enemy jets by detecting a plane's heat emissions. Naturally, it was named the Sidewinder missile.

For me as a film composer, I use my imagination everyday. When I begin working on the musical score to a film, I look at the movie without any music allowing me to first imagine what type of music will work with the film. Because there is no music at this point, I have a blank canvas to imagine without limitations. I want my creativity to be free and uninhibited where all options are possible. There are no wrong answers, only possible musical solutions.

I will watch a single scene multiple times, imagining different musical genres, styles and solutions. Before I begin composing the actual musical score, however, I *visualize* what the music will sound like and what instruments will play the notes. I *visualize* every detail of the score, every nuance of the sound, every color that I will use to grace the musical canvas of the film. I can "see" and "hear" the score in my mind long before it has been created.

You must imagine in the present moment.

In experiencing creative visualization, you must imagine yourself being, doing and having the outcome you seek. By imagining that you are experiencing this choice in the present moment, you are programming your subconscious mind to begin creating this new image or desired result.

For me, I visualize myself in front of the orchestra, conducting the piece of music I have not yet composed. This process prepares my mind for the actual work of composing the musical score. My mind is already preparing for the final outcome, and the resulting recording session has already been visualized before it occurs.

American music critic Arthur M. Abell published a book in 1955 titled *Talks with Great Composers*. As the Berlin correspondent for the Musical Courier, he conducted interviews with many composers including an interview with the prolific German opera composer Richard Wagner, who is known for his great works; *Tristan und Isolde*, the *Ring Cycle* and *Parsifal*. Wagner credits imagination for his creative process stating, "I have discovered that it is not will-power, but fantasy-imagination that creates. I see in my mind's eye definite visions of the heroes and heroines of my music dramas. I have clear mental pictures of them before they take form in my scores, and while I am holding fast to those mental images, the music, the Leit-motives (musical themes for each character), theme, harmonies, rhythms, instrumentation, in short, the whole musical structure, occurs to me."

"Imagination is the creative force, and this is true. I find not only of musical creations but also of external circumstances. For instance, after Liszt, with his successful production of my *Lohengrin* at Weimar in 1850, had revived my drooping spirits, I commenced work on the *Ring* and while composing the four music dramas, I conjured up distinct visions of a special Wagner Theatre, where they could be produced, an lo and behold, it became a reality! My imagination created it. Believe me, imagination creates the reality. This is a great cosmic law."

Mr. Abell's interview of Wagner continued by asking, "Does this only occur in music?" Wagner quickly responded, "Shakespeare, knew this law and he left records proving it. It was from him that I took my cue." Wagner went on to quote part of the fifth act, the first scene of *Midsummer Night's Dream:*

> Doth glance from heaven to earth, from earth to heaven;
> And as imagination bodies forth

The forms of things unknown, the poet's pen
Turns them to shapes, and gives to airy nothing
A local habitation and a name
Such tricks hath strong imagination.

Wagner shared an illustration of the power of imagination while composing his four epic musical dramas known as the *Ring Cycle,* "When I commenced work on *Rheingold* in 1853, I was lying in bed. I imagined myself lying at the bottom of the Rhine. I could certainly feel and hear the moving, surging water sweeping over. Musically, this took form in the shape of a chord. I felt the flowing of the Rhine as a figuration of that triad, surging incessantly with increasing motion."

"I was in a semi-trance condition and when I awoke, I immediately realized that this vision was an inspiration – that my prelude to *Rheingold* had taken shape in my inner consciousness."

The great artist and sculptor Michelangelo also knew how to visualize. All of his magnificent sculptures began as simple blocks of marble. He used his imagination to visualize his sculptures and statues within the block of marble to determine what that block of marble may become.

One of his most stunning and revered statues is the beautiful *Angel of Arca di San Domenico* located in the Basilica of San

Domenico in Bologna, Italy. He was asked how he could make such a marvelous model from a shapeless stone? He simply declared, "I saw the angel in the marble and carved until I set him free."

In Michelangelo's mind, this block of marble simply had a statue of an angel inside of it. He believed that it was always there, and he was able to visualize it within the block of marble proclaiming, "In every block of marble, I see a statue as plain as though it stood before me, shaped and perfect in attitude and action. I have only to hew away the rough walls that imprison the lovely apparition to reveal it to the other eyes as mine see it."

Allow your mind to *see* the results now.

Michelangelo could *see* the finished statue before he lifted hammer and chisel to marble just as you can *see* the desired results before beginning your process of change, innovation or creation. Even Pablo Picasso applied the process of visualization as he painted stating famously, "I paint objects as I think them, not as I see them."

By imagining in the present, just as these renowned artists did, you actually create the mental groundwork for your imagination to become reality. This process paves the way for your dreams to become your reality.

Unfortunately, this powerful use of imagination has become a lost art form among many people and many organizations. Like any skill, imagination needs to be practiced.

In Lewis Carroll's classic literary work, *Alice's Adventures in Wonderland*, Alice finds herself in a dialogue with the Queen of Hearts. "There's no use in trying," says Alice. "One can't believe impossible things." The Queen replies, "I daresay you haven't had much practice. When I was your age, I always did it for half an hour a day. Why, sometimes I've believed as many as six impossible things before breakfast."

With the chaos of daily life, little time is ever set aside to imagine impossible things. Yet, those impossible things can become tomorrow's innovative ideas and solutions, if we are priming the creative pump by deliberately exercising our imagination.

Why is it that we deem things to be impossible? Are they really impossible or have we simply resolved ourselves into believing they are impossible?

We must be curious.

The art of possibility means coaxing and cultivating curiosity. Becoming a curious innovator requires practice until it becomes a mighty skill. As children, we are all born with it. Most of us, however, have forgotten the skill we once practiced daily without even thinking about it. The Queen of Hearts knew the power of this practice. On a daily basis, we too must practice using our imagination.

I remember taking a child development class in college, many years before I had children of my own. One of our assignments was to observe children playing. We were positioned in a room outfitted with a one-way mirrored window where we could observe the children playing on a playground, yet they were completely unaware of us watching them. We were to take notes on the children's behavior, how they interacted with the other children and document their behavior. This was done for an hour once a week, over a series of weeks.

As I watched them, I was fascinated at how the children played together, as well as completely independent of one another. You could clearly see they were playing imagination games. The freedom that each child exhibited in how they interacted and how they used their imagination reminded me of the freedom that I too once exercised.

In the TED Talks video entitled *Build a School in the Cloud*, 2013 TED Prize winner and educator Dr. Sugata Mitra observed the power children have to explore and learn from each other in the experiments he called 'hole-in-the-wall'.

Dr. Mitra would watch children play in the slums outside his New Delhi office window. He then came up with an idea and proceeded to cut a hole between his office and the slum, giving these children access to a PC equipped with high-speed Internet and a touchpad for the children to interact with the PC. In a very short time, the young children began using the computer with no prior experience or knowledge of how to use it.

Dr. Mitra took the same experiment to other regions in India. Each time, he would leave a computer along with CDs providing no direct instructions on how to use them. To his delight, in a few short minutes the children were browsing the Internet.

When Dr. Mitra returned three months later to one of the experiment sites, the children exclaimed, "We need a faster processor and a better mouse." What was the most amazing is that these children did not even speak English! They had learned English from the CDs and in fact they were using approximately 200 English words with each other.

Dr. Mitra proved that children teach themselves and each other through simple curiosity. This curiosity fosters discovery and these children in India discovered this by way of his 'hole-in-the-wall' experiments. Children everywhere innately know this. We need only to remember for ourselves.

Remember: create curiosity

To do this you must imagine impossible things. I suggest going to visit a park where children play. Find a bench nearby, sit and watch the children play. Observe what they are doing and watch their joy in losing themselves in imaginative play and discovering. This flexes your visualization muscles, as you learn from their curiosity. You will be reminded of the creative curiosity that you *still* posses.

The Scottish novelist and playwright J.M. Barrie penned one of the most beloved stories about a mischievous boy, *Peter Pan*. Peter was known as the boy who wouldn't grow up. One of Peter's most enviable qualities was his ability to fly. Aided by fairy dust, Peter used his "lovely wonderful thoughts" to take flight. Even the Darling children took part in this wonderful experience of flight and they questioned, "Why can't you fly now, mother?" Her response was "Because I am grown up, dearest. When people grow up they forget the way."

J.M. Barrie's message profiles the great tragedy we experience as we grow up and forget the unlimited possibility of our youthful imagination. Peter exclaimed, "The moment you doubt whether you can fly, you cease forever to be able to do it."

Don't be limited to the possibilities of what may seem logical, safe or predictable.

Instead use your imagination. You have always possessed it. You have just simply forgotten how to use it. It's still there, hidden among the countless other things in your mind.

For those I train in my Directing Creativity workshops, I use an exercise for practicing imagination. Pretend you are a film composer like myself – composing scores and conducting orchestras. I'm not suggesting that you develop the skills to compose music, but I am inviting you to do what I do at the beginning of every project.

Watch a movie or television program with the sound turned down. You may not be able to determine what is going on in the scene and that's OK. Just use your imagination.

- Who are the characters?

- Is there a distinct emotion in the scene – Happy, tragic, suspenseful, romantic?

- What are the characters talking about?

- Where are they and is it past, present or future?

- What are they doing and why?

- How does the scenario end for each of the characters in the scene?

Once you have imagined their dialogue, become a film composer and don't worry if you are not musical. Imagine what type of music you hear that supports the scene in your mind. Use language and your experiences to imagine what type of music you think would work with the particular scene. It's OK to reference other pieces of music or other films. Do your best to imagine what the music would sound like and be specific.

- What genre of music would be used – Rock, jazz, classical?

- What main and supportive instruments are used?

- What is the speed or tempo of the music?

- As the scene changes, how does the music change?

- Is there a climax in the scene? If so, how does the music build and crescendo?

- How will the music support the ending scenario?

Once you have imagined the sound of the film, try imagining another type or genre of music that is completely different from what you previously imagined.

As you try this experiment, you will quickly see that you have the ability to imagine something that you really don't have any expertise in, and yet you will be able to imagine the music!

The opposite is a great exercise as well. In my training program titled *Ignite Imagination – Sparking Your Creativity*, we use the same process by listening to a piece of instrumental music by itself. Close your eyes and allow your mind to imagine a scene within the music. Describe this scene in detail.

- What do you see and what is going on in the scene?

- Are there people or a particular place in this scene?

- What is the time period – past, present, future?

- Is there a distinct emotion that comes into your mind?

- Is the scene action packed, romantic, dramatic, funny, scary?

Now imagine this to be a scene from a movie. As you are listening to the music track, use your imagination to create the scene. It can be anything you have in your imagination. Unleash your curiosity and let the music help inspire your imagination allowing you to set the scene free.

- Is there a particular plot that comes into your mind?

- How do the characters or objects unleash this plot?

- As the music ebbs and flows, what is happening in the scene and to the characters?

- Is there a climax in the music? If so, what is happening in the scene?

- How does the plot end – tragic, heroic, happy, sad, funny?

You can use the same imagination skills without movies and music. You can use these skills in your profession, in your organizations and within your teams. Again, close your eyes.

- Where will you or your organization be in 6 months, a year, 5 years?

- What new value can you offer?

- What products, services or solutions will you create?

- Where can you capitalize on current or future resources?

- What new value do you bring to the world?

- What do you imagine creating next?

Visualize your own success.

Practice like the Queen of Hearts to use your imagination each day. Begin your day imaging something impossible and in doing so, you will flex your mind's muscles. According to Oliver Wendell Holmes, "The human mind once stretched by a new idea never goes back to its original dimensions."

Imagination is the precursor to inspiration. Once you loosen the mind to the process of gathering impressions and possibilities you are *Directing Creativity*. This inspiration is the impulse that sets creation in motion and an energy that keeps it going. Imagination is your catalyst, the spark that ignites our imagination and starts the chain of events that lead to innovation.

The great statesman Winston Churchill said, "The empires of the future are empires of the mind." All innovation begins first with our imagination.

The outcome of imagination is *Inception*.

Inception is the beginning; start; or commencement. In science fiction, inception means the act of instilling an idea into someone's mind by entering his or her dreams. For the process of innovation, inception shares both meanings. Inception is the initiation of the creative process. It is the act of instilling, introducing and implanting an idea, both in *your* own mind and in the mind of others. Imagination begins the process.

Remember how you used that imagination as a child. *Remember* that your imagination knew no bounds. *Remember* how powerful you felt knowing that you could achieve whatever your mind could conceive. *Remember* that you are still capable of using your imagination. You are *still* an artist, capable of the art of all possibility.

CHAPTER 3

❖

BEHIND THE SCENES

The Creative Partner

As I sit in my studio watching a scene from a film I'm scoring, I imagine numerous musical solutions. Sometimes I arrive at what seems to be the *only* solution. When I allow my mind to work behind the scenes, additional and varied ideas will appear. Many times my instincts are correct and my initial idea was the right idea however, there have been many instances where *time* has provided a *better* idea.

Time and patience are the only way to permit the creative work to continue behind the scenes of our conscious efforts. If we hastily jump from imagination to execution, some critical nuances will be overlooked. Hidden details will remain covered and our creative objectives won't be able to fully realize their potential.

"One should never impose one's view on a problem; one should rather study it, and in time a solution will reveal itself." Albert Einstein knew what he was talking about, as solutions will reveal themselves but only if we allow them time to manifest.

Incubation is allowing for the work to be done *behind the scenes.*

Step 2 - *Incubate*

Taking time to think, to ponder, to reflect, to research, to evaluate, and to contemplate are all part of incubation. Skipping step 2 can be a crucial mistake in the process of creating a new idea, product or service. Many times we get so excited with igniting our imagination that we skip right over this step. Yes, imagination leads to the inception of innovation, but without following step 2 your imagination can lead you into unpredictable territory, derail the process of innovation and can lead you into a catastrophic direction or an ultimate course of defeat.

The Greek philosopher Plato also knew the importance of allowing for this work to be done behind the scenes in our mind. In the work *Phaedrus,* there is a dialogue about divine inspiration between Plato's main protagonist Socrates and Phaedrus where Phaedrus proclaims, "The mind ought to sometimes be diverted that it may return to better thinking." It's clear that Plato knew that incubation of ideas was critical to better thinking, thus better ideas.

Bill Hewlett, half of Hewlett-Packard (HP), was a great engineer and innovator. HP is the world's leading PC manufacturer specializing in developing and manufacturing computing, data storage and networking hardware, designing software and delivering services. However at its core, Hewlett-Packard is in the innovation business.

In order for HP to successfully innovate, Bill Hewlett understood the importance of step 2: *Incubate.* He recognized that most of our mental life is subconscious, even as much as ninety percent, and if we fail to make use of this mental power we will surely narrow our creative limits stating, "A period of gestation sets in, during which time things are mulled over. You put them in your mind and consciously or unconsciously work at them at odd hours of the day or night, even at work. It is somewhat analogous trying to place a name on the face of someone you've met before. Often the solution to a problem comes to you in much the same way, you eventually recall the name."

Incubation allows our minds the necessary processing time but only when our imagination has first set our thoughts free.

It is during this processing time when we will compute new connections and creative directions to consider against our initial ideas. Our minds will calculate and analyze possible pitfalls to avoid and can in fact, arrive at a clearer, more direct path to an innovative solution.

I absolutely love it when my subconscious works on my musical compositions when I'm not consciously composing. My brain knows what I need to create and it works overtime to assist me. It stimulates my composing through brilliant flashes of inspiration and even works when I'm sleeping!

I have discovered over these many years that patience is a necessary ingredient of inspiration and I certainly create better music if I allow my ideas time to incubate. The great composer Richard Strauss said, "Ideas, like young wine, should be put in storage and taken up again only after they have been allowed to ferment and to ripen." By giving ideas time to marinate they become richer, with greater complexity and depth. Often these ideas will take sidetracks that will lead to new discoveries, combinations and solutions.

I've learned to embrace this time of incubation. When the spark comes, I act quickly to capture it. As a composer I know that I'm not alone. Beethoven would take regular morning walks during which time he would allow his mind to come up with any sort of musical idea. He would take whatever the idea was and scribble it down in his pocket sketchbook. It didn't matter what the idea was or whether it was for a musical composition he was currently working on, he simply captured his subconscious ideas and committed them into his current conscious state.

Beethoven sketched constantly. His compositional process of sketching first set him apart from many of his contemporaries. He first began sketching on individual sheets, switching to sketchbooks in 1798. Those sketchbooks became Beethoven's sole creative vault of ideas. He used those sketchbooks to archive ideas and allow his subconscious time to work on them. He would jot down musical ideas, leave them and a few months later, take those ideas and transform them into larger ideas.

These sketchbooks housed themes for compositional ideas, musical fragments and plans for future works to be composed. You can follow the progress of Beethoven's musical ideas, through their various stages of development, until those ideas reached their final form.

The sketches for the *Quartet Op. 131* covers three times as many pages as the finished copy of the work. In his sketchbook covering his seminal work, the *Ninth Symphony*, there are no less than four variations of the *Theme of Adagio*. Each variation is a complete musical thought, but you can see Beethoven continuing to use the previous idea as a creative catalyst for the next version of the theme.

The melody may change directions, moving upward in a previous version and then moving downward in a later draft. Rhythmic durations and intervals of the melody would continue to evolve, as Beethoven continued sketching. With each subsequent sketch of the melody, he would build on the previous idea by enlarging it, expanding its musical scope and finally resulting in the creation of the finished melody of the *Ninth Symphony*.

Beethoven discovered the secret of capturing ideas in the moment, preserving them and allowing his subconscious to develop them over time. His compositional process was meticulous. He captured each musical idea in his sketchbook, but it was during the incubation period, the time between the musical variations, that Beethoven transformed those ideas into some of the most enduring pieces of classical music.

Consider the great composer Wolfgang Amadeus Mozart

in Edward Holmes' *Life of Mozart* where Mozart describes this process in his own words, "When I am, as it were, completely myself, entirely alone, and of good cheer – say, traveling in a carriage, or walking after a good meal, or during the night when I cannot sleep; it is on such occasions that my ideas flow best and most abundantly. Whence and how they come, I know not; nor can I force them. Those ideas that please me I retain in my memory, and am accustomed, as I have been told, to hum them to myself. If I continue in this way, it soon occurs to me how I may turn this or that morsel to account, so as to make a good dish of it; that is to say, agreeably to the rules of counterpoint, to the peculiarities of the various instruments, etc."

Mozart continues, "All this fires my soul, and provided I am not disturbed, my subject enlarges itself, becomes methodized and defined, and the whole, though it be long stands almost complete and finished in my mind, so that I can survey it, like a fine picture or a beautiful statue, at a glance. Nor do I hear in my imagination the parts successively, but I hear them, as it were, all at once. What a delight this is I cannot tell! All this inventing, this producing, takes place in a pleasing lively dream."

"When I proceed to write down my ideas, I take out of the bag of my memory, if I may use that phrase, what has been previously collected into it in the way I have mentioned. For this reason the committing to paper is done quickly enough, for everything is, as I said before, already finished; and it rarely differs on paper from what it was in my imagination."

Notice Mozart's process. He begins with imagination but allows time to incubate. Then his ideas flow quicker and clearer. For Mozart, those musical ideas rarely changed once committed to paper, demonstrating how much heavy lifting his subconscious actually did while working behind the scenes.

Both Beethoven and Mozart knew that their ideas had a very short shelf life and if they were not captured and committed to paper, they would fly away, never to be captured again. Even Thomas Edison would sometimes sleep on a table in his laboratory so that he could start work as soon as he awoke in an effort to not forget anything.

Therefore when you are in the process of innovating and flexing your creative muscles, prepare for flashes of inspiration as your subconscious arrives at solutions and bursts them into your conscious state of mind. *You must capture them quickly.* Don't rely on your memory, as you *will* forget the moments of inspiration if they are not recorded.

Whether it is a notebook and pen positioned on your nightstand next to your bed, or a recording device in your smart phone, you should never be without a way to capture those moments of inspiration. They will come. They will be magical.

Magical moments of inspiration are forgotten if not recorded.

On a recent film project, I was struggling to come up with a certain musical theme for two of the film's main characters. The theme was to be romantic but it needed to be subtle. I had many different variations and ideas yet none of them seemed right. They could work, but I knew there was something better, even perfect, that was yet to be discovered.

I went on to begin working on another part of the film. Then one afternoon it happened, that brilliant flash of inspiration that only comes to me from incubation. I was walking out of my studio and all of a sudden this four-note idea came to me. I began humming it to myself and quickly ran, yes I ran, to my piano. Being a seasoned composer, I knew that this was one of those magical moments of discovery. I couldn't take my time in hopes that I would remember the musical idea later. It had to be captured immediately.

I sat down at the piano and began playing the first four notes of the theme. Then, as if a blindfold was removed, I could see all the remaining notes. They flowed freely from my fingers, as the music literally appeared. My mind had been working on this piece for days now giving my subconscious time to continue working. And when it had arrived at the moment that my subconscious could contain it no longer, it burst onto my conscious mind. I was prepared to receive it and capture it.

Thomas Edison knew that he couldn't force the ideas he had until they were incubated and ready. His lab was a large barn equipped with worktables throughout the room where each table held a separate project in process. This allowed him the freedom to work on one project and then leave it to work on another. Time away from each project served as an incubation period until the creative solutions, moments of inspiration and even genius, would be discovered.

Incubation periods should exist to forget the obvious.

Try this exercise before you go to sleep tonight: Take a few minutes and review a current project, idea, or challenge in your mind. Write down some key words associated with it on a sheet of paper and put the paper next to your bed. When you awake, immediately look at the paper. What new insights do you have? Can you see more clearly?

You might even get one of those "sudden bursts of genius" moments. If you don't arrive at any new discoveries don't worry, it just means there is more work to be done behind the scenes. Don't force the revelation. The object of this exercise is to simply let it happen.

The American painter, graphic artist and sculptor Robert Rauschenberg whose early works paved the way for the Pop art movement, sought inspiration during his incubation periods. "For me art shouldn't be a fixed idea that I have before I start making it. I want it to include all the fragility and doubt that I go through the day with. Sometimes I'll take a walk just to forget whatever good idea I had that day because I like to go into the studio not having ideas. I want the insecurity of not knowing, like performers feel before a performance. Everything I can remember, and everything I know, I have probably already done, or somebody else has." What a great method for *Directing Creativity*!

While having been there before can stop you from finding new ways to get there again, there's always another way. Creativity always provides another solution. Henry Ford said,

"The air is full of ideas. They are knocking you in the head all of the time. You only have to know what you want, then forget it, and go about your business. Suddenly, the idea will come through. It was there all the time."

In Michael Ray and Rochelle Myers' book *Creativity in Business*, they tell the story of a Western businessman who had heard that a Zen master living on a faraway mountain knew the three secrets of life, and anyone who could obtain these secrets would know everything he needed to live a happy, fulfilling life. The businessman, whose life felt empty, reflected at length on what these three secrets might be. What possible words would answer all of life's problems and guarantee constant feelings of wellbeing?

Determined to find out, he finally sold his business and began his travels in search of the great master. Two years later, he arrived at the top of the right mountain and at the right zendo. There he sat … the Zen master.

The man approached the sage and said, "Oh, master, I have traveled far and wide to hear the three secrets that I need to know in order to live a full and rich life. Would you tell me those secrets?"

The master bowed in return and said, "Yes, I will tell you. The first secret is pay attention. The second secret is pay attention. And the third secret is pay attention."

If we pay attention at every moment during our incubation step, we will discover an enlightenment of ideas, and most often in these times those flashes come when you least expect them.

It's like when you shop for a new car. Once you decide on a make and model, you suddenly begin noticing how many of those same cars are on the road. It's not that there are actually more of the same cars driving around your neighborhood, it's just that you are more observant.

When we pay attention, incubation is enlightened.

Incubation does not mean simply waiting. Although the work being done in our minds behind the scenes might appear to be passive, we can actively help out our subconscious. It's working hard for us – the least we can do is encourage it.

This encouragement is found through searching. No I don't mean searching for more ideas, I mean searching for the ideas we already have imagined.

Werner K. Heisenberg stated, "The mere act of observing something changes the nature of the thing observed." This is the time to really dig deep into the ideas you have already imagined.

- Are there similar ideas that already exist?

- Have you imagined a new product or service that is derived from an existing product or service?

- Has your idea been tried before?

- If so, why did it succeed or what led it to fail?

A unique point of view is often found within existing points of view. We must search them out. Some call this our intuition.

The word intuition comes from the Latin word *intueri* meaning to 'look inside' or 'to contemplate'. The step of incubation gives birth to the process of allowing something 'inside' of us to process part of creativity.

Our intuitive subconscious can and will solve any problem for us if we know how to direct it. Again, this subconscious process is always at work. The question, are we simply passive observers of this activity, or are we striving to consciously direct our creativity?

Take for example when young eggs are placed in an incubator. They are carefully arranged to receive just the right amount of light to help them grow. For premature infants, an incubator provides the controlled conditions, like temperature, for their protection and care. The step of incubation provides the optimal conditions to foster maximum growth of our creative ideas. The incubation period might appear to be passive, but instead there is a great deal of work going on behind the scenes that we cannot see.

Use your periods of incubation to search, observe and nurture.

When I had the idea to begin this book, it was just that, an idea in my imagination. After I had imagined all of the wonderful things I would write, I needed to begin writing. However, I needed to follow my own steps – I needed to incubate the idea.

I first began formulating the ideas 18 months earlier. I observed my creative process as a composer very closely. I wanted to see exactly how I went about creating a musical score and once I could articulate those steps, I was ready to start writing, or so I thought.

I got busy composing a new film score and put the book aside for a couple of months. When I returned to it and began where I had left off, I had discovered something new.

The only way to describe it is to compare it to my most recent visit to my eye doctor. I wear glasses to read and after talking with the doctor, he had me tryout a number of new prescription lenses. I thought I could see, but when he would insert a new lens, I could now see more clearly. It seemed somebody had cleaned the window and my vision was sharper.

When I returned to my book, I was amazed at the new insight I had. I had figuratively put on a new set of glasses and now I could see it clearer! What I had originally set out to write in the book was now beginning to be altered, channeled more specifically and refined to a higher, clearer vision. I discovered so many new revelations about the creative process and began to see new connections that previously had been hidden.

Now that my own subconscious was really working behind the scenes, I did everything possible to keep it working. I would occasionally make a random observation about a particular concept and say, "That should be in my book!" Or "I never considered that before."

Simply because I gave my imagination time to incubate, the ideas and new insights were all around me. These new thoughts and insights came to me when I was writing music, NOT when I was writing my book. My subconscious knew it needed time to keep working on the book even when I was composing music.

Taking the time to incubate gives way for deeper understanding and more profound vision.

Vincent van Gogh said, "It is looking at things for a long time that ripens you and gives you a deeper understanding." Consider this deeper understanding from Li Li Weng's comment, "First we see the hills in the painting, then we see the painting in the hills."

As a composer, I can't begin writing until I have properly incubated my ideas. My best work has always been the result of properly incubating my initial concepts. In fact, I build into my writing schedule time for incubation. It may not always be as long a period as I would like, but I never omit this step. However short the writing schedule is, I never skip step 2 of the innovation process when creating a new musical score.

If I try and make up the time in my creative process by skipping this step, the end result will always suffer. My ideas will not have cohesion. It will actually take me longer to find the musical direction of a score because I will be searching for that direction while I'm trying to write. I will waste precious time in my very tight writing schedule for the delivery of a finished score on a film. However, when I ensure a period of incubation, my musical vision will always be clearer.

Let your ideas germinate. In so doing, you consciously make the decision to incubate your idea.

The outcome of incubation is *Insight*.

In *Directing Creativity*, don't skip over step 2. Incubate and let go of certainties. Allow this crucial work to be done behind the scenes with your creative partner – your subconscious.

CHAPTER 4

❖

EIGHTY-EIGHT KEYS

The Sketch

"He who deliberates fully before taking a step will spend his entire life on one leg." – Chinese Proverb

I sit in my studio watching a movie multiple times and imagine not only what the music might be, but I also visualize myself conducting the score. However there comes a time, with the deadline looming, I must begin *writing* the music. I can't think about it any longer and don't have time for any more mental considerations. With 70 minutes of music to write in 4 short weeks, and after imagining and incubating ideas, it is now time to get off one leg and take the step.

According to Picasso, "Inspiration exists, but it has to find you working." Thomas Edison said, "Genius is one percent inspiration and ninety-nine percent perspiration."

The great American author Jack London proclaimed, "You can't wait for inspiration. You have to go after it with a club." Leonardo da Vinci professed, "I have been impressed with the urgency of doing. Knowing is not enough; we must apply. Being willing is not enough; we must do."

Now is the time to stop talking, thinking and planning.

Step 3 - *Improvise*

To compose and perform or deliver without previous preparation is *Improvising*. Improvising is arranging from whatever is available. In music improvising is playing, composing, reciting or singing in the spur of the moment.

For me, step 3 is the most exhilarating step of them all. It is the step that holds the most surprises and reveals the most secrets. This step without question is the most rewarding.

A great example is the late Duke Ellington, an American composer, pianist and big-band leader. He composed over 1,000 musical arrangements that stretched across various genres including: blues, gospel, film scores, popular, and classical music. Rather than jazz, he called his music

"American Music" and is considered the primary musical figure that elevated the perception of jazz to an art form on par with the other traditional genres of music at the time. Duke Ellington was an innovator and many of his works have become standards in the music catalogs.

Ellington's compositional process follows step 3, *Improvise*. "I begin by tinkering around with some old tunes I knew. Then, just to try something different, I set to putting some music to the rhythm that I used in jerking ice-cream sodas at the Poodle Dog. I fooled around with the tune more and more until at last, lo and behold, I had completed my first piece of finished music."

The same process is revealed by one of the greatest violinists of the 20th century, Yehudi Menuhin, who not only played passionately the notes written on the page, he also knew the musical value of improvisation. "Improvisation is the expression of the accumulated yearnings, dreams and wisdom of the soul."

Creative ideas begin in the imagination.
Improvising gives birth to those ideas.

I love to improvise and when composing a film score, I always begin by composing the main thematic ideas first.

These themes will serve as the building blocks for the entire musical score.

Beginning at the piano, the themes are basic in idea. Whether the theme will be a sweeping, romantic piece played by a large string section, or large-scale action cues and heroic sequences, the process is exactly the same. I begin composing with the basic melody and harmony. Now these themes are born from improvisation. For a composer improvising is simply the process of musical brainstorming.

This brainstorming is the act of stimulating creative thinking and the development of new ideas. For the innovator, brainstorming is a free-flowing conduit of possibilities.

If imagination is the initializing of creativity, then improvising is opening the floodgates and grabbing every idea as it passes by.

This makes me think of the great California gold rush of the 1840s, where thousands of would-be-gold-seekers flocked to the region in hopes of striking it rich. Their process of mining for gold required that the miners use a pan, submerge it in water and shake it to sort the gold from gravel and other material. Since gold is much denser than rock, it quickly settles to the bottom of the pan.

For larger-scale endeavors, a sluice box would be used. Using a sluice box meant creating a channel with riffles set in the bottom. The riffles are designed to create dead zones in the current to allow gold to drop into them. The box is placed in the stream to channel water flow and much like the pan, a sluice box allows the gold to travel into the box and become trapped at the bottom.

Today this technique is still used, however instead of pans and small sluice boxes in rivers, large vacuum pumps suck up gravel, particles and gold from the bottom of the ocean and pump them through a more sophisticated sluice box. Once the flow of water is stopped from the sluice box, gold nuggets and tailings remain trapped in the bottom.

Improvising is like panning for gold. Much like the miner, we as innovators begin looking for that single gold nugget in a river of possibilities. As a composer, I too pan for that musical idea that will provide the framework for my score. The question is how do we stumble upon the gold?

Thomas Edison said, "To have a great idea, have a lot of them."

Much like in the step of *Imagine,* the key to *Improvise* is to remove all parameters. The more open you are to free-flowing creative ideas, the more creative solutions, or gold nuggets, you will discover. Don't limit your ideas to only good-sense suggestions. Instead allow every idea the same consideration. Picasso said, "The chief enemy of creativity is good sense."

Disney Imagineers follow the principle of "blue sky speculation," a process where Imagineers generate ideas with no limitations. The custom at Walt Disney Imagineering has been to start the creative process with what is referred to as the "eyewash" – the boldest, wildest, best idea one can come up with, presented in absolute convincing detail. Many Imagineers consider this to be the true beginning of the design process and operate under the notion that if it can be dreamt, it can be built.

Sketching is the mechanism to give birth to ideas or dreams.

A sketch is a drawing intended to serve as the basis for your finished product. It is a rough draft, design or plan. Its purpose is preliminary, giving the essential features without the details. Sketching is the most active, unrestrained step of the innovation process and where ideas begin to take shape, while moving them from your thoughts to reality. Sketching is the only way to transform concept into product.

For me, the process of sketching is captured by improvisation. I sit at my piano before 88 keys and begin playing, hunting, pecking, searching and scratching for something that sparks my interest. It might be a chord progression, a simple motive, a hook of a few notes, or maybe it's a rhythmic phrase. Regardless of what manifests, I am completely immersed in the search. I don't know what I'm going to discover, but if I continue to improvise I know I will find something.

Once I get that small seed of an idea, I move to my composing station of computers, electronics and most important the movie, where I might improvise as the scene plays. I always have my sequencer recording the notes because I never know what idea might surface. Most importantly, I remain totally open to any idea.

I have discovered that much of the improvisational process is an intuitive one. I react to the film and go with my gut reaction to the drama by only concerning myself with the emotion it evokes. While the pacing of my improvising might be completely off, and I certainly will hit a lot of wrong notes in the process, I don't mind because I'm musically brainstorming. There will be plenty of time later to sort it all out. I'm searching for ideas, lots and lots of ideas.

This process will continue until I feel I've got an arsenal of material. This material will become the building blocks for the musical score. I will still have to construct the plan or sketch, but right now I'm just looking for the blocks.

While sketching ideas, improvising solutions or brain-storming strategies, you must not allow yourself to have any pre-conceived notions. You have to be totally objective about the process.

Thomas Edison was notorious for his tough interview questions for would-be applicants wanting to join him at his Menlo Park lab. Many of the 150 questions posed to applicants were not targeted specifically to the industry, but rather to test the applicants on their general knowledge of many divergent topics. Many of the questions were random and mysterious. Then if Edison felt the interviewee was a strong candidate, an invitation to dinner would be extended.

Unaware, the candidate's interview would continue over a meal. When the food arrived, Edison would watch carefully if the applicant seasoned or salted the food prior to tasting it. If the candidate would season the food prior to tasting it, he never had a chance for employment. Edison did not want people who had built assumptions without first hand knowledge or experience. He wanted to be surrounded by those who would not make general assumptions and was looking for people with an open mind, those who would look at problems with a fresh approach. Edison wanted individuals with no preconceptions, people who would allow their minds to remain open for any and all ideas to be considered.

We must always remember that nothing kills creativity more quickly than critical, judgmental thinking. It's easy to judge, evaluate, or criticize ideas during improvisation and sketching. Don't do it and defer your judgment. No squelching of any ideas! As we improvise, there are no wrong ideas. Winston Churchill proclaimed, "No idea is so outlandish that it should not be considered."

It's OK to suggest an idea that will never work, is too expensive or is completely irrational. Many great ideas come from radical notions. So don't worry about suggesting a crazy idea. There will be ample time later to consider, sort and select the best ideas to use. Instead, be like the sluice box that takes in everything. Once the flow of water stops, then you can look to see what gold you really have.

Unfortunately, too many of these creative brainstorming sessions are viewed simply just another task, event or meeting. I can assure you that they are not and should be treated special with proper preparation. Before you begin your improvising or brainstorming session, ensure you have no distractions and that enough time has been allocated to the session. Don't let interruptions like phone calls, emails and other disturbances get in the way of your creativity. When I'm improvising, the door of my studio is closed to the outside world. The phone is turned off. My full attention is given to the improvising step in the creative process.

Another consideration is to encourage participation from a broad spectrum of opinions. Don't always rely on the same group of people around you or in your organizations to generate new ideas. Mix it up! By inviting a diverse group of participants, you will get a true cross-section of ideas.

In an organization, invite lower-level staff to contribute equally with upper-management. Brainstorm with many different and diverse talents. Divide into smaller groups by gender, work experience, departments, geographic regions, education and so on. Have each group brainstorm and then bring the groups together to share their ideas and to look for ways of combining them.

It is important to recognize that too many times we brainstorm until we think we have arrived at some good ideas and we stop before the great ideas come.

Sketching is active. It is aggressive.

One powerful exercise I enjoy doing when I speak to audiences is called Idea Quotas. I ask the group to look at the stool I have on stage and then I ask them to come up with 101 uses for the stool. We won't stop until we reach 101 uses for the stool.

At first the ideas will flow easily. As the group gets closer to the quota of 101 uses of the stool, the uses become more difficult to identify. It would be easy to stop around use number 57 because honestly, the group has identified more uses for the stool than anyone would ever consider. Yet I won't let them stop. We won't stop until we reach 101 uses.

In this exercise, quantity breeds quality. Audiences discover that in many cases the later ideas are the best ones.

- Do not stop brainstorming until your reach your quota.

- When it becomes tough to come up with another idea, dig deeper.

- Change your perspective – there are more ideas just below the surface.

- Don't concede victory to a few good ideas so quickly, keep searching – there will be more waiting to be discovered.

- Keep scratching, improvising and brainstorming until you discover them.

In Michael Michalko's book *Cracking Creativity*, he describes this type of thinking as *thinking fluently*, or to be more precise, "distinguishing characteristic of genius is immense productivity." In other words, have lots of ideas!

Thomas Edison held 1,093 patents, which remains a record. He guaranteed productivity by giving himself and his assistants, idea quotas. His personal quota was one minor invention every ten days and a major invention every six months. Bach wrote a cantata every week, even when he was sick or exhausted. Mozart produced more than six hundred pieces of music. Einstein is best known for his paper on relativity, but he published 248 other papers. T.S. Eliot's numerous drafts of "The Waste Land" constitute a jumble of good and bad passages that eventually was turned into a masterpiece. Rembrandt produced around 650 paintings and 2,000 drawings and Picasso executed more than 20,000 works.

Now once you have your supply of ideas, sort them. Identify those ideas of immediate usefulness. Put the other ideas in a category for further exploration along with those that could provide new approaches to the problem.

Consider everything as you improvise.

In my work, I have composed many musical ideas that will never end up in the movie. However, if they are not right for this film, it doesn't mean they won't be right for another film. Do not throw away your unused ideas. Keep them. Cherish them. Guard them. They are nuggets of gold. You never know when that unused idea will be just the right solution for a future problem.

As I am composing a score, I am constantly referring back to my sketches from my improvisation sessions. Even recently when I was working on a film, there was a particular sequence that I had written three different version of music for, but none seemed to be working. I was nearly finished with the film and couldn't seem to find the right musical solution.

I went back to my sketches that I had written at the very beginning of the film during my improvising process. There it was, one of the very first ideas I had composed. I had completely forgotten this musical idea, yet there it was, the musical answer I had been seeking.

I quickly played the melody along with the film and it was perfect! Every nuance I had been searching for was right there in my original sketch. I had composed the perfect solution long before I encountered the musical problem.

While there are so many musical gems waiting to be used, and some of them never make it into the score, they will remain ready to go for the next project. Even if some of my ideas seem like they will never be used I don't discard them for they may provide a launching pad for future ideas.

The outcome of improvisation is *Intention*.

There's a wonderful Japanese proverb that says, "Vision without action is a daydream. Action without vision is a nightmare."

Now that all of your ideas have been sorted, categorized and accounted for, you have your building blocks of innovation. These organic ideas will transform your sketch into a working blueprint, a plan for *Directing Creativity*.

CHAPTER 5

❖

TUTTI

The Full Score

A blind boy sat on the steps of a building with a hat by his feet. In his hands he held up a sign that said, "I am blind. Please help." But there were only a few coins in his hat. A man walked by and noticed the boy and his hat. Taking a few coins from his pocket, he dropped them into the hat and took the sign from the boy, turned it around and wrote some words. Putting the sign back so that everyone who walked by would see the new words, soon the hat began to fill up. More and more people passing by were giving money to the blind boy.

That afternoon, the man who changed the sign returned to see how things were going. The boy recognized him from his footsteps and asked, "Were you the one who changed my sign this morning? What did you write?"

The man replied, "I only wrote the truth. I said what you said but in a different way." The sign now read, "Today is a beautiful day and I cannot see it."

While both signs told people that boy was blind and that they could help by placing money in the hat. The second sign encouraged the passers by to appreciate the beauty of the day, however, the young boy cannot enjoy seeing it because he is blind.

Although the boy was creating a revenue stream from his hat, it wasn't until the collaboration of the passing man that the revenue quickly increased.

Collaboration is the act of working together with others.

Step 4 - *Integrate*

Innovation requires creating in tandem with others. In music, *Tutti* means: all voices or instruments playing together. Mastering this art of collaboration will produce better innovation.

The playwright George Bernard Shaw said, "If you have an apple and I have an apple and we exchange these apples then you and I will still each have one apple. But if you have an idea and I have an idea and we exchange these ideas, then each of us will have two ideas."

As a film composer, I love this sentiment because I know the importance of sharing, collaborating and integrating ideas. After I have been hired to compose a new film score, I immediately begin the art of collaboration. This starts by asking lots of questions of the director, as my job is to extend his vision for the film. It is my responsibility to translate his emotional and dramatic direction into music. After all, as the director, he cannot fully innovate and execute the creation of a movie without collaborating with his team.

"Great discoveries and improvements invariably involve the cooperation of many minds. I may be given credit for having blazed the trail, but when I look at the subsequent developments I feel the credit is due to others rather than myself." Even the great inventor Alexander Graham Bell felt that although he might be the main inventor, his success was dependent upon others.

Integration and Collaboration is not a solitary exercise.

Every movie has a spotting session where the composer, the director, the producer(s) and any other creative execs offer input to the musical direction of the score while all are convened together to watch the film. I love spotting sessions, because it is the time when we all get to integrate our ideas together.

Before any spotting session takes place, I have to read the script, see cuts of the film and, in many cases, even started the composing process. I have already imagined, incubated and improvised ideas before this meeting.

Now together with all of the creative people involved we get to make collaborative decisions about the music. We discuss where there will be music, what the music will do in the scenes, how large a scope the music will play, and we discuss if the music will be melodic, rhythmic or atmospheric. Many times the director or producer will use other pieces of music to communicate with me in musical terms. We determine when the music will crescendo and when it will drop back behind the dialogue or other key moments of a scene, talk about the use of popular songs in the film and discuss the sounds of the musical score. In short, everything musical is discussed.

These spotting sessions generally take a long time because each scene in the film is discussed in detail. This is the time to integrate all of the creative ideas into one cohesive plan. This step of collaborative integration provides me with the comprehensive plan for composing the musical score.

The step to *Integrate* is key to moving along the innovation process. It flows in both directions from the director's creative vision to my musical contribution and back again. The philosopher Thomas Carlyle said, "The lightening spark of thought generated in the solitary mind awakens its likeness in another mind." The light has now been sparked in all of our minds.

I can now return to my studio to compose. Here I will continue the process of *Directing Creativity*, or sometimes I will begin again from step 1 until I, once again, reach this step of *Integrate*.

I will then meet again with the director and producer in my studio where we preview the movie with the initial music I have composed for the film. This is where adjustments are made in collaboration before we go into the larger recording studio to record with an orchestra.

At this stage there is a great deal of collaborating taking place. Even though I am hired to create an original score for the movie, it has to be the score that the director and producer envision. If I refuse to integrate both my ideas with those of the director and producer, I will not be on the film much longer.

There are countless stories in Hollywood of creative egos battling over the direction of a movie. The great films, and certainly the great filmmakers, know that without collaboration they are all doomed.

No idea, no creator, no executive, no ego is too big to *Integrate*.

Henry Ford was considered one of the greatest innovators of the 20th century. Contrary to popular belief, Henry Ford did not invent the automobile. Although the Ford Motor Company did produce the vehicle that initiated a new era in personal transportation, the Model T, the invention of the first automobile is generally credited to Karl Benz of Germany. In reality to this popular belief, Henry Ford's most important contribution was actually the invention of the moving assembly line.

Prior to Ford's invention, factory employees would work in groups building one car at a time. By inventing and installing a moving assembly line in his factory, workers instead began to build cars one of three thousand pieces at a time in 84 distinct steps – with each individual responsible for a specific job along the path.

With the integration of the world's first automatic conveyor belt, Henry Ford's factory in Michigan was soon producing a car every 93 minutes versus one every twelve hours. It was his new process of integration throughout an entire factory that gave Ford the ability to revolutionize the production of cars more efficiently and expeditiously.

It was in the late 1920's when the Asian rubber importers of the Far East had a monopoly on the rubber industry and Ford's hundreds of thousands of new cars needed millions of tires. He was losing leverage in negotiations with the importers. At the time, America was consuming more than 70 percent of the world's rubber, with most of it going to Detroit and Ford's factories.

Ford had seen British rubber companies take Amazonia rubber trees to Asia where they established massive rubber farms. Ford decided to take matters into his own hands and established *Fordlandia*, a tiny piece of America transplanted into the Amazon rain forest for a single purpose: to create the largest rubber plantation on the planet.

In 1929, Ford bought 2.5 million acres of land in the Amazon along the banks of the Rio Tapajos. He set off to create an entire city that would be dedicated to producing rubber and inhabited by 10,000 people. He built housing for the workers, a pool, tennis court and even a golf course. There was a hospital along with a library and hotel. *Fordlandia* was slated to be a booming community.

At this time, Ford had experienced great success with his production lines for manufacturing cars in Detroit and believed the success of the model would apply to production of rubber trees as well. The formula for success seemed eminent, however, Ford had no botanists, geologists, forest engineers or agricultural specialist in *Fordlandia*.

He enlisted trusted and skilled engineers who calculated the production of rubber trees like calculating any other math problem. They calculated against their target of 38,000 tons of rubber a year and determined they would need more than a million trees. This meant planting them seven feet apart along crowded rocky hillsides. Ford and his team naturally assumed that planting more trees would yield a larger amount of rubber required to fulfill their goals.

Over the first year, the tiny *Fordlandia* saplings were not growing well. The hilly terrain where the trees were planted struggled to hold its topsoil, as the irrigation would wash it downhill. To make matters worse, only seven rubber trees grow naturally in one square acre of land in the Amazon rainforest. At *Fordlandia*, they were trying to grow 200 trees in a square acre.

The close proximity of the trees proved to be a perfect incubator for predatory insects and disease. Whatever small growth did occur in the young trees, tree blight and insects would quickly devour the fresh leaves leaving the rubber trees stunted and unable to thrive. Not realizing the cause of the tree's lack of productivity, Ford continued stripping and clearing more rocky Amazon landscape and planting tree after tree.

In 1931, a British journalist from the *Indian Rubber Journal* visited *Fordlandia*. He wrote, "In the long history of tropical agriculture, never has such a vast scheme been entered in such a lush manner and with so little to show for the money. Mr. Ford's scheme is doomed for failure."

Finally in 1933, Henry Ford hired a botanist to assess the situation. The botanist tried to rid the trees of the leaf blight that loved the location of the damp, hilly terrain of *Fordlandia*. The botanist ultimately concluded that the land was simply unequal to the task. In the end, *Fordlandia* would never produce a single piece of rubber worthy of Ford's cars.

Henry Ford's plan failed to include the integration and collaboration with botanists, rather than engineers, and ultimately cost him 200 million in modern dollars. What a costly loss from such an innovate mind! Had Ford integrated and collaborated, he might have succeeded in producing rubber.

Creative collaboration is the key.

IBM calls this creative collaboration 'partnering for profitability.' In a recent study conducted by IBM among chief information officers to discover the effects of integration in the innovation process, IBM's research teams found that when organizations chose to partner for outsourcing rather than the typical do-everything-in-house approach, they discovered much greater success at innovation. At the same time, and contrary to this study's findings, more than two-thirds of the CIOs revealed that they are focused more on internal collaborations.

Consider IBM's recommendations to these CIOs after conducting the study; "Enable state-of-the-art collaboration. Evaluate and adopt new tools to strengthen enterprise-wide collaboration and real-time exchange of data ... Increase two-way transparency by involving diverse staff in decision-making."

Even after 25 years as a composer, I am always amazed at the finished product as I collaborate with my team. The creation of the musical score is far better than if I had skipped this step of integration.

The recording session is my favorite part of the process, precisely because of the collaboration with many people.

I allow for everyone, including the musicians playing the scores, to participate in the creative process. Even though they are reading the notes of the page that I wrote, they are bringing their own expertise to the performance. As I stand on the podium to conduct them, they are breathing their own identity into the music. Their years of practice and interpretation on their instruments integrate perfectly into my vision of the musical score.

You can see it as clearly as I do, that for me alone I cannot create a finished movie score. I need the integration of talented musicians, recording studio staff, orchestrators, music copyists, music editors, recording and mixing engineers and other key staff to assist in the realization of what I had imagined alone in my studio.

What Henry Ford failed to remember at *Fordlandia*, he initially learned back in 1913 when the first assembly line was implemented at the Ford Motor Company. This is what Douglas Brinkley profiled in his book *Wheels for the World: Henry Ford, His Company, and A Century of Progress*. He showed how the assembly line process grew like a vine and eventually spread to all phases of Ford's manufacturing, and ultimately throughout the entire world of heavy industry. "There can be no doubt that a powerful revolution had occurred – but it was not the assembly line itself that provided the power. Rather, it was the creation of an atmosphere in which improvement was the real product: a better, cheaper Model T followed naturally. Every man on the payroll was invited to contribute ideas, and the good ones were implemented without delay."

Foster a culture of collaboration.

In my work, I deliberately create the cultures and environment, which begins as I collaborate together with the director of the film, keeping cognizant of the fact that it is his or her film. I am being hired to contribute to the whole film and not being hired to compose a concerto where the music is the star, standing out from the actors or other collaborators. I am part of the entire film's tapestry and together, the director and I seek to find the music that is perfect for the film.

This collaboration process continues when I work with my orchestrator. I have composed the music and created electronic versions of the music for the director to listen to alongside the film. Now it's the orchestrator's job to take my music and create the full-score from which each instrument's individual part will be extracted, prepared and printed for the recording session.

I rely on my orchestrator to catch my mistakes, make creative suggestions and truly participate in the realization of the score, knowing my music will be better by collaborating with him. The recording sessions go much smoother, as a second-set of eyes have poured over the scores.

Composing, orchestrating and recording with the musicians are all part of the integration process to deliver the final score. And now, as I stand before the orchestra ready to lift my baton to commence, if I have not successfully gained the collaboration of all the musicians the result will not be very enjoyable to hear. I rely on each one of them, as my notes on the page are integrated through the interpretation of their individual and collective performances. I need their full buy-in to assist me in creating the musical score for the film.

Once all of the music has been recorded, I now have another step of integration with my engineer, as we work together to mix the music. I know what I want the music to sound like but I certainly don't have the technical expertise that my engineer has. I need his creative input to mix the score together.

From the mixing studio, I take the music to the dubbing stage where together with the dialogue and sound effects, the music is mixed together for the final time with all of the other sound elements.

There are three dubbing engineers, each charged with either the dialogue tracks, the music tracks or sound effect tracks. In the end, there are hundreds of individual audio tracks to be mixed together for the film's final mix that the audience experiences in the theater. The director, producer, executives and mixing engineers are all gathered together for this final step in the integration process.

Can you see how vital integration is to the innovation process? Without it, I would still be alone in my studio imagining how wonderful the score might be. Yes, I can do a lot alone in my studio, but it is impossible for me to do it all. The art of collaboration is required and there is a great byproduct from collaboration, as I get pushed, pulled and stretched to go in directions I might never go otherwise. I discover ideas and solutions that alone would have remained hidden.

Collaboration is key to successful innovation.

All great leaders of innovation know that *Directing Creativity* is a true team effort. The great Michael Jordan certainly knew this, "Talent wins games, but teamwork and intelligence wins championships." The secret to real team effort and measured success is collaboration!

Pixar, the animation studio who brought us *Toy Story, Monsters Inc., Finding Nemo* and *The Incredibles,* as well as many other great, animated films, has always known the value of integration. Collaboration is critical to Pixar's strategy and it even changed the company's mission with its creative development teams. Instead of 'coming up with new ideas for movies', which is a common approach in the industry, their job became 'to assemble small incubation teams that help directors refine their own ideas into powerful visions' that can then be presented to the management board.

Consider some of history's greatest creative innovators that we generally regard as solitary geniuses. In reality, they were great collaborators and understood how integration was key to their success. Historian William E. Wallace discovered that thirteen people collaborated with Michelangelo on the Sistine Chapel masterpiece. Around two hundred people assisted the master on the Laurentian Library in Florence, Italy.

In the modern world of art, Pablo Picasso and Georges Braque, by combining their talents, invented cubism an early 20th century avant-garde art movement. Cubism revolutionized European painting and sculpture, and inspired related movements in music, literature and architecture. Perhaps either one of them working alone might have invented it. But without question, when the two combined their talents and integrated their ideas, their contrasting talents inspired cubism's paradoxical properties.

Throughout my career, I have had the good fortune of working with many different directors. No two were alike. The directors that I enjoyed the best were those that understood collaboration. Some directors had no idea what they wanted and looked to me for all of the answers. While, unfortunately, others would have composed the score themselves if they could have. Due to the fact that they were incapable of writing the score on their own, they would dictate to me every note and tie my creative hands. The directors that gave both general and specific direction, those who sought my creative opinions and then collaborated on the final musical score, understood the power of integration. I stretched my own creativity to match the vision of the director and those directors received a far better musical score for their film.

Each and every time a director truly wanted to integrate an idea, we each emerged with more than we began with, and the result was far superior than we could have achieved alone.

Collaboration broadens creative vision.

While visiting Florence, Italy, and because of my obvious interest in the great creative masters, I made it a point to seek out some of the finest marble sculptors of the Renaissance. None are more famous or spectacular than Michelangelo and his masterpiece *David*. This great work of art is considered by some to be the most perfect depiction of a man ever chiseled from stone. *David* has become a symbol of both strength and youthful beauty.

It was fascinating to view *David* from different sides and angles. From the front he stands poised for battle. From the left side the detail of the veins from his hand bulging forth dominated the view. Looking into his face David portrays innocence, yet looking from another angle you see his sling flung down over his shoulder. He is perfect in every way, yet different from each vantage point.

The art of collaboration is much like the statue of *David*. We cannot see the entire thing from one vantage point. Instead, we observe it by moving around the statue, beginning with one particular view and, taking in all the elements, eventually come back to the starting point where we again see the original view but in a new profound way.

Not only have we viewed the statue from different angles, each viewer takes with them a unique memory from the viewing, forming an opinion about the statue. When they return to the beginning of the statue, each recalls different impressions that stand out to them. Integrated together, all of the ideas accurately portray the perfect beauty of Michelangelo's *David*. We now see and appreciate *David* from all perspectives.

Collaboration provides multiple perspectives.

Leonardo da Vinci understood this and believed that in order to gain knowledge and solve a problem, you had to first learn how to restructure it to see it in many different ways. He would look at his problem from one perspective and move to another perspective and still another. Leonardo da Vinci called this *saper vedere* or "knowing how to see."

For the end product of a musical score to be a success, my entire team needs to share the same vision, we must 'know how to see'. The only way for this to occur is if together we can integrate ideas, talents and abilities.

In the end we must all have the same desire, to see the beauty of the statue. We all must strive to foster this attitude with everyone that will share in the innovation process. Be inclusive, not exclusive. Consider the advice from the great basketball coach Phil Jackson, "The strength of the team is each individual member. The strength of each member is the team." The immortal college basketball coach John Wooden, simply stated the universal truth, "Everything we know we learned from someone else."

Keep in mind that integration also applies to the combination and collaboration of your ideas. After sketching covered in chapter 4, you may be left with divergent ideas. Try integrating some of them together. Remember what Thomas Edison did in his lab where all his worktables were scattered about and how each table would hold a separate project and was designed to allow one project to affect, influence and inspire another project? Edison was constantly rethinking, reworking and re-evaluating each project, by integrating with another project.

Integration provides combinations.

This can be seen in the German blacksmith, goldsmith, printer and publisher Johannes Gutenberg's integration of divergent ideas that gave birth to the printing press in 1448. He did this by combining the mechanisms for pressing wine and punching coins, creating movable type. His method endured almost unchanged for five centuries.

By making combinations, perceptions are changed. Einstein did not invent the concept of energy, mass or the speed of light. Instead, he meaningfully combined these concepts to become useful. By combining the concepts in a different way, he was able to look at the same information and see something different.

There are only twelve notes in the musical scale. It is the integration, arrangement, sequence and combination of those twelve notes that forms music. In my search for the perfect melody, I seek to find just the right combination of those twelve notes, integrating melody, harmony, rhythm and counterpoint resulting in a finished piece of music.

The outcome of integration is _Illumination_.

Whatever your creative endeavor, embrace integration and collaboration. More light will illuminate, broadening your vision, allowing you to see clearer – the full score.

CHAPTER 6

❖

EDITING ROOM

The Lift Off

"If you wish to advance into the infinite, explore the finite in all directions." This was profound advice given from the 17th century German writer, artist and politician Johann Wolfgang von Goethe. Albert Einstein believed that "to raise new questions, new possibilities, to regard old problems from a new angle, requires creative imagination and marks real advance in science." One of my favorite quotes is from the great 20th century Russian composer Igor Stravinsky who said, "I have learned throughout my life as a composer chiefly through my mistakes and pursuits of false assumptions, not by my exposure to founts of wisdom and knowledge." Maybe Thomas Edison said it best:

"There's a way to do it better – find it!"

Step 5 - *Inspect*

What all of the great creators agree upon is this final step in the innovation process. In the making of a movie, I have discovered a microcosm of steps within this step; inspection, improving, rewriting, re-editing and reworking.

To begin this process, the script is rewritten until it works on a story-level, as well as to accommodate the budget. Then the editors make assembly cuts of a film. They proceed to inspect and rework these edits from the assembly cut into a rough cut, then into a fine cut and finally arriving at a picture-lock version of the film.

As the composer, I begin composing with broad thematic ideas. Then I rework those thematic ideas to match the picture-lock version of the film. I will ultimately rewrite individual music cues to match the exact mood and feel the director desires.

In thinking over my body of work as a composer, I'm confident saying that the final music scores were almost always better after this step of inspecting, reworking and rewriting. As a matter of fact, there has never been a film finished without these rewrites.

When Mozart composed, he would begin with the large structure of his musical composition – its shape and basic dynamics. After having reworked the overall structure, Mozart would go back and adjust and refine his musical composition in fine detail. This process of inspecting what he had composed, and then refining it, would reveal new ideas and would inspire him with new musical dimensions. Many times this would evolve into a completely new piece. He would then integrate the new ideas into the composition's tapestry that would arise.

This was part of Mozart's genius. It was not always discovered in his first ideas, but rather in his revisiting and inspecting his initial ideas, and refining them into the musical compositions that have stood the test of time.

Creativity stops where you decide to end it.

The discipline of inspecting what we have created and then editing that creative material is a tough step. It can be hard to look at what we have created objectively, without any emotional attachment and see how it can be better. Rare is the occasion that we create perfection without any revisions.

In fact, creativity does stop where *you* decide to end it. Too many times we think we have "arrived" at the answer, solution or invention. If we press in and apply the final step in the innovation process, the step to *Inspect*, we will discover more creative solutions and products are waiting to be discovered.

As I continue rewriting music, this inspection process first begins by myself – critically examining and revising the compositions. Once I feel I have arrived at the best musical choice, the director and producer now offer their feedback. From these various inputs, there are additional music rewrites and changes in where the music fits in the film and other "creative" decisions based upon this conscious step of inspecting.

I am not alone in the rewriting process. Even John Williams, the legendary Hollywood film composer whose career has spanned over six decades garnering him 50 Academy Award nominations and an unprecedented collaboration with Steven Spielberg, must also contend with these rewrites.

During the time he was composing the score to the movie *Close Encounters of the Third Kind*, John Williams wrote over 300 examples of the iconic five-note theme for the alien spaceship before director Steven Spielberg final chose the one that ultimately became the film's infamous motif.

Consider the story that best describes this process of inspecting and refining is seen with two of the worlds' greatest inventors, Orville and Wilbur Wright, as profiled by Mary Bellis in her article *History in Flight – The Wright Brothers*. The year was 1899 and the Wright Brothers had spent a great deal of time observing birds in flight. They noticed that birds soared into the wind and that the air flowing over the curved surface of their wings created lift and the brothers believed they could duplicate the structure of these wings.

Over the next three years, Wilbur and Orville would design a series of gliders, which would be flown unmanned as kites, but more importantly be flown piloted.

They took full advantage of step #2 *Incubate,* as they gained greater *Insight*. The brothers read and studied about the great works of Cayley and Langley's hang-gliding flights of Otto Lilenthal. They then corresponded with aviation pioneer and engineer Octave Chanute concerning some of their ideas. Step #4 *Integrate,* led them to *Illumination*.

Following the building and successful testing of their glider, the Wright brothers built and tested a full-size glider with the goal of manned flight. They selected Kitty Hawk, North Carolina as their test site because of its wind, sand, hilly terrain and remote location.

In 1900, the Wrights successfully tested their new 50-pound biplane glider at Kitty Hawk in both unmanned and piloted flights. With its 17-foot wingspan, this was the first piloted glider to ever be flown in history.

Based upon the results, the Wright Brothers planned to refine the controls and landing gear, and then went on to build an even bigger glider. In 1901, at Kill Devil Hills, North Carolina, the Wright Brothers took to flight the largest glider ever flown.

With a 22-foot wingspan, a weight of nearly 100 pounds and skids for landing, many problems occurred. In a moment of profound disappointment Wilbur Wright confessed, "Man would not fly for 50 years", predicting that man would not fly in their lifetime.

Embrace the process of Inspection.

In spite of the serious problems with their last attempts at flight, the Wrights went back to *Inspect* and reviewed their test results. They determined that the calculations they had used were not reliable, which led them to further *Illumination*.

With this inspecting and improving, they decided to build a wind tunnel to test a variety of wing shapes and their effects on lift. Based upon these tests at close range, the inventors had a great understanding of how a wing worked and could calculate, with greater accuracy, how well a particular wing design would fly.

Through improving upon earlier models, they now planned to design a new glider with a 32-foot wingspan and a tail to help stabilize it. In 1902, the brothers flew numerous test glides where these studies revealed that a movable tail helped to balance the craft. The brothers then connected a pivoting tail that would coordinate turns. With further inspections verified by wind tunnel tests, the inventors planned to build the world's first powered aircraft.

After months of studying how propellers work, the Wright Brothers designed a motor and a new aircraft that was sturdy enough to accommodate the motor's weight and vibrations. The craft weighted 700 pounds and came to be known as the Flyer. The brothers also built a portable track to help launch the Flyer. This downhill track would help the aircraft achieve the speed necessary to gain lift and fly.

After two attempts to fly this machine, one of which resulted in a minor crash, Orville Wright took the Flyer for a 12-second, sustained flight on December 17, 1903. This was the first successful, powered, piloted flight in history.

Inspecting leads to refining and perfecting.

Thomas Edison is often credited as the inventor of the light bulb, but he did not actually invent the light bulb. Rather he improved upon the idea of 22 other men who pioneered the light bulb before him.

Nikola Tesla, a Serbian American inventor, engineer, physicist and futurist, was best known for his contributions to the design of the modern alternating current (AC) electricity supply system. During the late 19th century, Tesla took the principle of AC current, that was developed by Michael Faraday, and improved, refined and perfected it. This innovation is still in use today.

Guglielmo Marconi, an Italian inventor, is known for his pioneering work on long-distance radio transmission. His first transatlantic radio signal in 1901 began his celebrated achievements and culminated into a shared Nobel Prize for Physics in 1909. Marconi succeeded in making radio a commercial success by innovating, improving and building on the work of previous physicists.

As Henry Ford said, "Simple genius is the ability to create something new from the ideas and inventions of others." Whether those new ideas come from other ideas, or from looking closer at current ones, the step to *Inspect* not only provides improvement but new ideas, concepts and products that are waiting to be discovered.

Many of us know of the Wright Brothers success of the first powered flight. Not as many are aware that they continued to discover more and more improvements, as they continued to apply the step of inspection. On November 9, 1904, the first flight lasting more than five minutes took place, the Flyer II, was flown by Wilbur Wright.

On July 30, 1909, the U.S. Government bought its first airplane, a Wright Brothers biplane. The airplane sold for $25,000 plus a bonus of $5,000 because it exceeded 40 mph.

In 1911, the Wright's Vin Flz was the first airplane to cross the United States. The flight took 84 days stopping 70 times. It crash-landed so many times that little of its original building materials were still on the plane when it finally arrived in California.

In 1912, a Wright Brothers plane, the first airplane armed with a machine gun, was flown at an airport in College Park, Maryland. The airport was built in 1909, during the time when the Wright Brothers delivered the first government-purchased airplane. They used this location to teach Army officers how to fly. On July 18, 1914, an Aviation Section of the Signal Corps, a division of the Army, was established. Its flying unit contained warplanes made by the Wright Brothers.

By inspecting their initial invention of the glider, the brothers made improvements that were nearly unimaginable in only a few short years. The Wright Brothers stand as a glowing example of the value that innovative contribution brings into our world by not skipping over step #5 *Inspect.*

Improvement requires heavy lifting.

It comes as no surprise that I have always been fascinated with Wolfgang Amadeus Mozart, as he was one of the most prolific composers in history. As a child prodigy, he wrote his first composition at age five and ended up composing over 600 works. He is among the most enduringly popular composers of the classical period, who even influenced Beethoven. Joseph Haydn wrote "posterity will not see such a talent again in 100 years."

The Academy Award winning film, Amadeus depicts the composer as, "A genius who writes as though touched by the hand of God." The film's story is told from the point of view of Mozart's peer, Antonio Salieri, who believed that Mozart was God's divine creative vessel.

Picture Mozart simply writing music spoken to him by Deity! It is an extraordinary image. Divine inspiration? Yes, I believe this to be real, but nobody worked harder than Mozart.

Consider Twyla Tharp's account of Mozart's work ethic in her book *The Creative Habit*:

Nobody worked harder than Mozart. By the time he was twenty-eight years old, his hands were deformed because of all the hours he had spent practicing, performing, and gripping a quill pen to compose. That's the missing element in the popular portrait of Mozart. Certainly, he had a gift that set him apart from others. He was the most complete musician imaginable, one who wrote for all instruments in all combinations, and no one has written greater music for the human voice.

Still, very few people, even those hugely gifted, are capable of the application and focus that Mozart displayed throughout his short life. As Mozart wrote to a friend, "People err who think my art comes easily to me. I assure you, dear friend, nobody has devoted so much time and thought to composition as I. There is not a famous master whose music I have not industriously studied through many times."

Mozart's focus was fierce; it had to be. In his relative short life, he endured conditions we can relate to like; writing on the road and delivering scores just before the curtain went up, dealing with the distractions of raising a family, and the constant need for money. Whatever scope and grandeur you attach to Mozart's musical gift, his so-called genius, his discipline and work ethic were its equal for him to deliver the music that he did.

It's clear that Mozart knew the importance of heavy lifting. He put in the time. The result? In his short 35 years of life, Mozart amassed a staggering creative output of operas, oratorios, concertos and symphonies.

Directing Creativity requires lots of heavy lifting, as great innovations don't just suddenly appear. It is through industrious qualities; work ethic and discipline that those who innovate are separated from those who don't.

Throughout my career, I have worked hard to create the scores I have composed. I've spent countless hours honing my skills as a composer, yet still I find myself struggling, scratching and clawing at creativity to discover the notes for my movie scores. It simply isn't easy. It's hard work.

The great football coach Vince Lombardi said, "The price of success is hard work, dedication to the job at hand, and the determination that whether we win or lose, we have applied the best of ourselves to the task at hand."

For each of us, the task at hand is different. For me it's composing a new melody, finding the perfect chord and not missing my recording date. For you it will be the task of whatever creative challenge you are facing. Lose yourself in the search. Bury defeat and self-doubt and do the heavy lifting to reveal the discovery.

Your unwavering commitment to the innovation process will grow your creative muscles. Henry Ford used to always say, "You can't build a reputation on what you're going to do." In other words, do the heavy lifting. Don't talk about it, don't think about it, and don't ask others to do it for you. Use Nike's famous tagline: Just DO IT. Walt Disney simply said, "The way to get started is to quit talking and begin doing."

As a composer myself, I am naturally drawn to the stories of other composers. I've referenced Mozart, who many believe is the greatest composer of all time. However, Johannes Sebastian Bach certainly deserves much credit. He was a German composer, organist, harpsichordist, violist and violinist regarded arguably as the most prolific composer of the Baroque period. His creative output is staggering: the Brandenburg Concertos, the Mass in B minor, The Well-Tempered Clavier, more than 200 cantatas, two Passions and other keyboard works. In total an eye-popping 1126 compositions.

ALAN WILLIAMS

Bach succeeded as a composer only because of his industrious efforts and doing the heavy lifting confessing, "I was
obliged to be industrious. Whoever is equally industrious
will succeed equally well." The great composer Schumann
said of Bach, "Music owes as great a debt, as a religion owes,
to its founder."

During his 27 years as the Director of Music in Leipzig, his
creative workload was immense. Each Sunday and Holy Days
of the year required a cantata, as well as other cantatas for special occasions. Nearly all of these cantatas were Bach's own
compositions, written weekly. Day in and day out, Bach did
the heavy lifting. His job was to create. Composing on de-
mand became second nature for him. With no time for writer's block, Bach simply wrote every day. Creating became a
part of his persona, yet his success he wholly attributed to his
work ethic.

Like Mozart and Bach, many innovative giants are viewed
as "geniuses endowed from God." But like Mozart, most
"creative geniuses" simply have learned the value of doing the heavy lifting. As Albert Einstein has said, "I know
quite certainly that I myself have no special talent. Curiosity, obsession and dogged endurance, combined with self-
criticism, have brought me to my ideas." Notice the ideas
didn't come to him. The industrious work brought Einstein

to his ideas. I encourage you: Stay the course. Do the heavy lifting.

The outcome of *Inspection* is *Improvement*

The innovation process is cyclical. As ideas are generated and solutions are discovered, the process restarts. Remember to always embrace the process of inspection.

Seek to discover not a good product, service or solution, but the very best product, service or solution imaginable! Good is the enemy of great. Strive for greatness.

CHAPTER 7

❖

RED CARPET

The Summit

We've all seen it: the red carpet. It's the holy grail of achievement, the pathway of stardom. Celebrities and VIPs all walk the red carpet. Photographers jockey for the best vantage point to snap iconic photos of the year's who's-who and which stars are wearing what designers. For the Academy Awards show, extended television coverage is graciously given, as Hollywood icons arrive and walk down that infamous red carpet.

I've walked the red carpet for award shows for which I have been nominated and for world-premieres of films for which I've composed the music. For me, the red carpet represents a pinnacle of purpose – the celebration of innovation completed.

It's not the actual red carpet, the glamour or the press circus covering it, but is the time to applaud the accomplishments of all associated with the creation of a movie.

A world-premiere is the final unveiling of coordinated creativity. After weeks, months and sometimes even years, a movie finally has its celebrated opening. All of the collaborators are gathered to celebrate the completion of their *Invention.*

The outcome of *all* 5 steps is *Innovation.*

From dream to reality, a tangible product has been invented. In this case, it's simply the assembly of all of the pre-production, filming and post-production elements compiled together onto a single piece of film. All of the dialogue from the actors, all of the sound effects and the musical score have been mixed together in perfect balance, now resulting in a single audio track married to the images on film. The movie is now a finished work of creativity.

Finally crossing the proverbial innovation finish line is certainly grounds for celebration and Hollywood does it in lavish style, with all of the glitz and glamour.

While your invention, and its unveiling to the world may not command such pageantry, doesn't birthing an idea into reality warrant some sort of jubilee? Pat yourself on the back. Give in to all of the accolades your peers are heaping upon you.

Go ahead and celebrate!

But by all means don't get too comfortable. Once the premiere is over and the lights come up, the discussion and debates begin. Was this invention groundbreaking? Can the world live without it? What about the skeptics and critics?

All creations, films or otherwise, receive bad reviews. All movies have critics that review and scrutinize every aspect of the film. In many cases, we, the movie-going public, even decide on viewing a movie based solely on its reviews. How dare someone else critique another's creative work? Yet there will always be a voice, maybe from the boardroom, maybe from the competition that is poised to stand up and shout from the rooftops the absurdity of your creation. Consider the following critics' assessment:

> "Everything that can be invented has been invented."
> -*Charles H. Duell, Director of the US Patent Office 1899*

> "Sensible and responsible women do not want to vote."
> -*Grover Cleveland, 1905*

> "Who the hell wants to hear actors talk?"

-Harry M. Warner, Warner Bros Pictures, 1927

"There is no likelihood man can ever tap the power of the atom."
-Robert Miliham, Nobel Prize in Physics, 1923

"Heavier than air flying machines are impossible."
-Lord Kelvin, President, Royal Society, 1895

"Ruth made a big mistake when he gave up pitching."
-Tris Speaker, 1921

"The horse is here today, but the automobile is only a novelty – a fad."
-President of Michigan Savings Bank advising against investing in the Ford Motor Company

"Video won't be able to hold on to any market it captures after the first six months. People will soon get tired of staring at a plywood box every night."
-Daryl F. Zanuck, 20ᵗʰ Century Fox, commenting on television in 1946

"What use could the company make of an electric toy?"
-Western Union, when it turned down rights to the telephone in 1878

"This 'telephone' has too many shortcomings to be seriously considered as a means of communication."
-Western Union internal memo, 1876

"I think there is a world market for maybe five computers."
-Thomas Watson, chairman of IBM, 1943

"We don't like their sound, and guitar music is on the way out."
-Decca Recording Co. rejecting the Beatles, 1962

And finally,
"Inventions have long since reached their limit, and I see no hope for further development."
-Julius Frontinus, highly respected engineer in Rome, 1st Century A.D.

Jean Sibelius, the Finish composer and violinist, had a prolific career that spanned from the end of the 19th Century to more than half of the 20th Century. As composer and violinist, Sibelius was frequently exposed to reviews and critiques of both his compositions and performances. He never allowed negative reviews to stifle his creativity, rather he would shrug away negative criticism by saying, "Pay no attention to what the critics say. A statue has never been erected in honor of a critic!"

Don't allow critics, skeptics, or past failures to get in the way of your commitment of creating. Sometimes the critics are correct – so use their assessment and return to the innovation process and create something better. Creativity always finds a better solution.

Besides the critics lining the red carpet and those waiting to squash our innovative solutions, whether publically or in the boardroom, there exists another critic. This critic is more powerful, persuasive and persistent than any contingency of press. This critic is our own self.

Self-doubt, personal critiques and self-evaluation are all natural in the innovation process, and we have learned that inspection leads us to improvement. Prolonged inspection can become paralyzing. We have given in to the strongest critic – self.

Embrace the critic.

I love Dr. Seuss. Whether it was *The Cat in the Hat, Green Eggs and Ham* or *How the Grinch Stole Christmas,* as children most of us remember a Dr. Seuss story and surely have our personal favorites.

As a writer, Dr. Seuss was open to the same personal-critic we all are subjected to. He realized who controlled the critic inside of him:

You have brains in your head.
You have feet in your shoes.
You can steer yourself in any direction you choose.
You're on your own.
And you know what you know.
You are the guy who'll decide where to go.

Dr. Seuss

Only we can control our personal critic. Ultimately, we choose.

As the African proverb says, "When there is no enemy within, the enemies outside cannot hurt you." How do we do it? Self-doubt is natural. How can we silence this critic within?

The great basketball player Kobe Bryant said, "I have self-doubt. I have insecurity. I have fear of failure. We all have self-doubt. You don't deny it, but you also don't capitulate to it. You embrace it."

Embracing self-doubt is like embracing our fears when we began creating. It is the same voice, trying mightily to discourage our creative efforts. The voice exists, so to control it takes embracing it.

In William Shakespeare's play *Measure for Measure*, the character Lucio shares with each of us the affects of our own self-doubt. "Our doubts are traitors, and make us lose the good we oft might win, by fearing to attempt."

As a composer, it is easy for me to "fear to attempt" in my creative process. Deadlines do help me begin the process of writing, but as I compose I am constantly evaluating every note I write. Is it the right melody? Can I write something better? Is the music any good?

If I am not conscious of the critic inside of my head, the voice can derail my own creativity by questioning every note I compose, giving way to paralyzing self-doubt and stopping my ability to create. One way I silence the critic in my head is to create in spite of the voices.

The great post-impressionist painter Vincent van Gogh would paint even when there was no inspiration. He would force himself to stay with his canvas, not giving into the temptation to stop. "If you hear a voice within you say, 'You cannot paint,' then by all means paint, and that voice will be silenced."

We may temporarily silence the voice by painting, composing or any other creative act. In short order, however, the self-critic voice will search for other ways to begin whispering in a new script, taking over and once again discouraging our innovative efforts. The act of creating will silence the voice, at least for a time, but anticipate the voice at some point down the road to return.

Recently I gave my first TEDx talk. It was an invigorating experience and the excitement surrounding the event was fantastic. Of course, I felt pressure to deliver my message flawlessly to the world. I spent many hours preparing, practicing and perfecting my talk. Then the time came to for me to deliver my message of *Directing Creativity* with the world. I boldly took to the stage prepared to pour out my message.

When I finished my talk, I immediately left the stage feeling like it could have been better. Rather than seeing the glass half full, my inner voice, the critic lying in wait to discourage all of my accomplishments, began screaming at me that the glass was neither half full nor half empty. In fact, the glass was now shattered into hundreds of pieces, with liquid residue spilling all over the floor. The voice knew that my talk was good yet it knew it was not perfect. The voice looked for any angle to criticize my message and the delivery.

For the public that attended the event, the enthusiastic applause told me that my talk was perfect. From talking with attendees following my speech, all appearances were that they enjoyed it immensely. But to me, I felt much like the playwright Tennessee Williams. "I don't believe anyone ever suspects how completely unsure I am of my work and myself and what tortures of self-doubting the doubt of others has always given me."

It is OK to hear the voice of self-doubt. It is natural for all of us. For a period of time after my speech, I not only heard the voice of self-doubt, I believed it. Regardless, we must not allow it to paralyze and consume us. This will halt creativity. I had to overcome it and you must as well.

Conquer the critic.

When overcoming doubt, I'm reminded of the explorer Sir Edmund Hillary and his Nepalese Sherpa, Tenzing Norgay, who set out to become the first climbers to reach the summit of Mount Everest, the tallest mountain on Earth. It required a team of hundreds, and enormous planning to attempt such an endeavor.

Upon finding themselves nearing the top of Everest, a crippling snowstorm and high winds held up Hillary and Norgay at the last camp for two additional days. They were just short of reaching the summit with only 1,128 feet separating them from the top of the mountain, yet the external conditions made the 29,028-foot peak seem miles away.

On the morning of May 29, 1953 the two climbers made the final 40-foot ascent named the "Hillary Step." At 11:30 AM Edmund Hillary and Tenzing Norgay finally reached the top of the world.

For Hillary, the challenge of summating Everest was not just the snow and wind, or the mountain itself. One of the greatest obstacles may have been overcoming his personal self-doubt. "It is not the mountain we conquer but ourselves."

Like Sir Edmund Hillary, we can exclaim that we too have conquered our own Everest. This overcoming of self-doubt will lead each of us to the top of the mountain of innovation and creativity. Once atop that peak, the view will be breathtaking.

Now from the top there can be a very slippery slope, as with any success the self-confidence may give way to the dangers of arrogance and ego. There must be a healthy balance between fear and doubt, and self-confidence. Healthy fear and doubt will help us push onward and upward in our creative quest, while excessive self-confidence may give way to arrogance and ego.

Be ever so careful to balance these two voices. Neither voice should reign supreme. The two can encourage you without overtaking your emotions, letting the voice of self-doubt and the voice of self-confidence balance each other out. Allow self-criticism to only lead you towards healthy improvement, without slowing your creative journey. Allow your self-confidence to celebrate accomplishments, as long as it is with humility.

Directing Creativity demands bravery and stamina. Just as we summit the mountain of creation, innovation will require your resolve. Consider Ralph Waldo Emerson's encouragement, "Whatever you do, you need courage. Whatever course you decide upon there is always someone to tell you, you are wrong. There are always difficulties arising, which tempt you to believe that your critics are right. To map out a course of action and follow it to an end requires some of the same courage, which a soldier needs. Peace has its victories, but it takes brave men to win them."

Don't allow the critics of creativity, inside or outside, to curb innovation.

Courage is essential to direct creativity.

"Success is not final, failure is not fatal; it is the courage to continue that counts." This was Winston Churchill's motto and he lived it. During the Second World War, it was his steadfast refusal to consider defeat that was evident in the early days of the War when Britain stood alone among its neighboring European countries in opposition to Hitler. He had a decision to make, give into his critics and surrender or create a compromise of peace? His answer helped to inspire the British resistance and preventing the imminent invasion of Britain.

Christopher Reeve, the original Superman said, "A hero is someone who, in spite of weakness, doubt or not always knowing the answers, goes ahead and overcomes anyway."

Conquer, summit and overcome the critics. Allow self-doubt to be your catalyst of action rather than inaction and permit self-confidence only enough space in your life to humbly celebrate your successes. As George Bernard Shaw said, "You see things; and you say, 'Why?' But I dream things that never were; and I say, 'Why not?'"

Creating a new paradigm, innovating a new product, or pushing against the status quo with a new philosophy will always be met with opposition. Don't let the storms of opposition from within or the noise from outside diminish your quest.

Innovation takes determination.

Despite the challenges of creation, and all of the critics that surround the process, climb to the top of the peak no matter the struggle. Take confidence that every step you take draws you closer to your summit of success.

Once you decide to exercise your creativity, there will be those who will try to discourage you. There is pessimism and speculation, regulations and protocol, budgets and timelines, but all of these need not stifle creativity.

Put on your best attire and smile bright for the camera. Walk the red carpet with your head held high. Celebrate the accomplishment of creation. Regardless of what the critics say, you have succeeded!

Burn this image into your mind and celebrate the red carpet moment. Relive it with confidence. Whatever the negative energy may be that waits for your future creative efforts; you have successfully stockpiled an abundant supply of fuel for future innovation. The critics no longer have influence over you. Push forward with purpose, boldly climbing the creative mountain ahead.

CHAPTER 8

❖

DIRECTING CREATIVITY

The Tactics

The culminating event for my work as a film composer is to stand in front of a symphony orchestra. The rush of euphoria, leading 100 musicians who are playing in complete synchronicity, creating a lush and powerful sound, far exceeds most of the other emotions I've felt in my lifetime.

Assembled before me in the recording studio are some of the world's finest musicians. Lingering overhead are priceless microphones strategically poised to capture the most delicate of sounds. Throughout the studio are the engineers and technicians who are eager to skillfully record the orchestra's performance.

I have stood on the podium countless times. Yet each time I raise my baton there is anticipation and an emotionally charged payoff when the musicians begin to play.

This emotion is so powerful that I once had a director refuse to leave my side at the podium because he too was so moved by the orchestra.

While standing at the podium, I am literally *Directing Creativity*. Leading, guiding and conducting the musicians through the endless streams of notes in the scores, I am encouraging them to play with greater intensity and sensitivity. I am coaching them with all the passion I can muster. I'm with them on every note to deliver a performance for the ages.

This is *the* essence of *Directing Creativity*. This *is* creativity and innovation fully realized. From the inception of my imagination, I'm now directing my creativity in a very real sense.

Anyone can experience this same euphoria by following the innovation process. It is this inception of the creative process that leads us to the end result that fuels even more creativity. The great American poet Maya Angelou said, "You can't use up creativity. The more you use; the more you have."

Create the perfect climate for creativity.

The right conditions need to be present for creativity to thrive. In his book *Creativity and Its Cultivation*, Erich

Fromm suggests there are certain conditions necessary in a perfect climate for creativity.

- The ability to be puzzled.

- The ability to concentrate.

- The ability to accept conflict and tension.

- The willingness to be born every day.

- To feel a sense of self.

Each and every one of these conditions exists when I'm in the recording studio. However, they are also present from the very beginning of my creative process as I embark on a new film score.

Each condition must be present in our quest for innovation and each needs to be encouraged, embraced and exercised for creativity to prosper. You must cultivate these conditions, even when you are not actively striving for innovation. The result will be creative insight.

Negative energy, however, is not part of this ideal climate. Remember the critics from the red carpet? Distance yourself from them. Be bold, daring and convicted, as you cultivate these creative conditions.

Creativity has an insatiable appetite.

Creativity needs nourishment – lots and lots of nourishment! So how do you feed your creativity?

To begin, you have to feed your own creativity first before you can encourage others to join the innovation process. Feeding personal creativity requires a daily diet of stimulation.

Feeding your personal creativity can occur in many ways. My own creativity is sometimes sparked as I absorb the creativity of others. Collaborating, discussing, sharing and integrating ideas are all important aspects of feeding creativity, because ideas take shape in the minds of others. I have gained a significant amount of creative-currency from spending time observing, associating and connecting with people from various walks of life and with creative people from other disciplines, industries and backgrounds. This exchange of ideas has also proven to be very fruitful in feeding my own creativity.

It was not long before I wrote this book that I was leading a creativity and innovation workshop with some top executives from a well-known entertainment company. Isolated from the noise of day-to-day business, together we delved into the innovation process. The team assembled and the conditions were intentionally ripe for creativity.

As we discussed and practiced the step of *Improvising,* I suddenly realized a solution to a marketing challenge I had been facing as a composer. There it was, in this shared creative environment! As we sketched and brainstormed solutions together, one of many possible answers to the company's challenge surfaced and was the exact answer I had been looking for.

Creative stimulus is all around us.

I love to travel abroad. Changing my environment by visiting other people and places feeds my creativity. Mingling among other cultures shines new light on my personal creative thinking and I discover new perspectives. Whether it is marveling at the architecture, expanding my experiences through local conversation or tapping into treasures of a new emotional response, by way of the region's art, music or cuisine, broadens my personal experiences and boosts my creativity.

While traveling on speaking tour in Curacao and Aruba that I was able to arrive at the creative insight for this very book! On these islands I found myself removed from the distractions of normal everyday life. Although I was there to speak about creativity, interestingly enough, it was by being in a different place, immersed in a different culture, and having these new experiences I was able to see clearly the need for this body of work to exist.

A few years ago my wife and I visited Petra in the southern part of the country of Jordan. I was fascinated with the stunning architecture of the ancient Arab Nabataeans. Their craftsmanship, detail and creative achievement were truly manifested in the striking and long-enduring monuments. Petra was a feast of creative culmination. However, it was not until I returned to Petra the next evening to visit *The Treasury* at nighttime that my true creative inspiration occurred.

To get to the *Treasury* required walking the Siq or narrow passage for nearly a mile, illuminated only by candles. In the distance we could see a yellow glow growing brighter as we reach the end of the Siq unveiling the iconic *Treasury*.

This great edifice was spotlighted by hundreds of candles from the ground, casting a glow of light high atop the creative masterpiece. This great architectural wonder had stood for more than 2,300 years. Now illuminated only by candlelight, the *Treasury* acted as a natural amphitheater for a lone Bedouin musician playing regional songs on his rababa, a crude Jordanian traditional violin.

As I sat on ground atop a locally hand-made rug, my senses were ripe for all creative stimuli. The imagery, sound and mysticism were intoxicating. Never had I experience something like this before. I suddenly began thinking of an upcoming film assignment and how I could incorporate various ethnic instruments and sounds into the film.

As the Bedouin musician continued playing, my mind continued to imagine, conceive and visualize many other projects and applications. I consciously committed the sounds to memory so that I could recreate the emotions from that evening in my studio on future projects.

This event broadened my experiences and ultimately gave way for greater creative vision. I found myself conceiving an album project in my mind influenced by these and other sounds from around the world.

You needn't travel halfway around the world to have this similar creative enlightenment. Cicero said, "Art is born of the observation and investigation of nature." Simply get out and take a walk. Listen. Observe. What do you hear? What do you see? What do you smell?

Consider some of these suggestions to feed your creativity, whether you are beginning the innovation process or stalled somewhere along the way:

Try striking up a conversation with a stranger. What new insights do you gain? Go to a new restaurant and order something you have never had before. Now talk with others at your table about what you enjoyed about your new meal. What surprised you the most about it?

Whenever Einstein would come to a difficult problem with work, he would listen to the music of Beethoven and Mozart, and the music would exhilarate and help him resolve his problem. So try listening to a piece of classical music. How does it make you feel? Try and articulate your feelings by describing how your emotions may have changed throughout the piece of music. What in the music caused you to shift your emotions?

As these exercises identify, new ideas will come at different times and in various forms during your innovation process. Ensure that this process continues regularly and without interruption, as regular feeding of creativity is required. As you will discover, this is accomplished through both active and passive activities.

Consider challenges in a new way.

Einstein said, "The gift of fantasy has meant more to me than my talent for absorbing positive knowledge." By feeding, creativity encourages your ability to tap into and release your unconscious and preconscious thought. Seek out avenues to a richer fantasy life and more involvement in daydreaming, and be impulsive.

Sometimes this creative fantasy or daydreaming can be fostered or fed by considering the opposite of it.

Try:

- Eliminating the specifics and focus on the generalities.

- Eliminating both the specifics and generalities.

- Overlooking details or remove an element, step or attribute.

Now ask yourself:

- What remains?

- How is it different?

- What new insights do you have?

Envision you are a stranger to the problem, never hearing of the problem before. It is now completely foreign to you. Imagine you are standing *outside* of the challenge looking *inside* at the challenge. What do you see?

You can also try feeding your creativity by collaborating with a divergent entity. Look outside of your normal creative circles. Consider inviting new contributors, especially those with varying degrees of experience and expertise. Try to mix up the demographics, as diversity always provides greater perspectives. What is the same in these collaborations?

To cultivate this creativity:

- Start at the end and work backwards.

- Go to the edge ... Now go further.

- Turn it upside down.

- Consider old ideas.

- Change the order and speed.

- How are the dots connected?

Combining various opposites may yield even broader results. Bottom-line? Forget the rules, color outside of the lines, throw away the box and, in some cases, restart. Never forget along the way to avoid the noise, as you must be still to focus and meditate.

Go to a park, sit and observe. Now close you eyes. What do you see? What do you hear? What do you feel? What do you imagine? Let go of your thoughts and allow your mind the freedom to dream. What fantasy fills your thoughts? Can you feel your creativity being fed?

Whether you love art or not, visit a museum and check your preconceptions and prejudices at the door. Open your entire being to this new experience. Submit to all of your senses and begin exploration. If you look for the inspiration in other's creative handiwork, you will come away from this visit inspired.

Go to the best sources to feed your creativity, as the best creative inspiration ensures the best creative return. Listen to the best composers, visit the greatest architectural buildings, view the greatest works of art and read from the best authors, beginning with the masterpieces.

Search for the best material to inspire you. Sculptors search for the best piece of stone before chipping away at the excess material. It's all in the material. I seek out the best musicians to perform my scores. The better the musician, the better my score will be.

Seek out creative-building experiences and get excited rather than guarded when confronted with new ideas. Be sure to change your routine, as *Directing Creativity* yields *Innovation*, which is the ability to see change as an opportunity, not a threat. Embrace this change.

Directing Creativity from all directions.

In Japan, Konosuke Matsushita, known as the "God of Management", was born into humble circumstances in the Japanese village of Wasa, Matsushita. At age 16, he went to work for the Osaka Light Electric Company. He excelled at his job and worked hard on creating a new type of light socket that was better than anything on the market at the time. Matsushita showed his invention to his boss, who was unimpressed.

So, in 1917, Matsushita left his job at Osaka Light. With the help of his wife and three eager assistants, he began his own business manufacturing his new invention. Slowly his new electric plug caught on and by 1922 his company was introducing new products every month.

Matsushita Electric continued to expand, acquiring many other companies even through the struggles of World War II when Matsushita's company barely managed hold on. In

1952, Matsushita Electric offered consumers the first black and white television sets and by 1960 his company marketed its first color television.

Matsushita Electric Industrial Corporation changed its name in 2008, based on the company's best-known brand Panasonic. At one point in time, any video tape recorder from GE, RCA, Sylvania, Magnavox, Montgomery Ward, Quasar or Panasonic, were made by Matsushita.

Unlike his first boss at Osaka Light, Konosuke Matsushita knew the importance of *Directing Creativity* from all directions. "A person who can create ideas worth of note," said Matsushita, "is a person who has learned much from others." Certainly a lesson his first boss could have learned. Matsushita took this mantra, and his invention, and embarked on a journey of his own. He always valued creative input from others and creativity was directed at Panasonic Corporation by this principle.

Matsushita's management philosophy and hence the title, "God of Management", is based on the following seven principles:

"Exceed customer expectation in products and services."

Make it a quest of discovery for this enlightenment to serve others and even society at a higher level. Ideas for over-delivering against others expectations of us can only be found as we search out new creative approaches. These ideas will not be found in the same place we have always found our previous ideas. Overturn every rock, look in all directions and be willing to be exposed to everything new and different.

> *"Achieve customer satisfaction and corporate profit through motivated, capable, informed and focused employees."*

Would my recording sessions achieve their full potential unless we are all playing from the same piece of music, as well as all motivated by the same ultimate vision? Of course they would not. This is no different with any other creative endeavor. We all must be playing from the same piece of music, moving in the same direction, with the same visionary goals.

> *"Perform professionally, ethically, and with the customer's interest in mind at all times."*

My job as a composer is to serve the movie and the director, not to seek out an opportunity to compose my personal works. While the screen credit says, "Music by Alan Williams" and will exist for the life of the movie, which will long outlive myself, I must remain true to the film and its director. It has to be my best, ethical work because my name is attached to it. You too are known for your works regardless if you receive public credit or not so always strive to be your best ethical and creative self.

> *"Establish long-term partnerships to enhance customer values and drive loyalty."*

There is a reason why in Hollywood that directors will continue to work with the same crews and even cast members over and over again. Loyalty, values and vision are to be shared, embraced and celebrated together. Once a creative team works successfully together, that team is reassembled time after time because of the shared partnership and loyalty that gives creativity room for, and ultimately enhances, the process and final product. This creative currency, creative collaboration and a vision of innovation should never be hidden in some back room or corner office.

> *"Invest in the future."*

Investing in the future means growing and feeding creativity. It also means looking for other creative avenues that may not be directly related to your field. For example, as a composer I not only write notes. Sometimes I write ideas through words, completely unrelated to music, just as some actors paint. We all must invest in our creative futures by seeking out other creative outlets to motivate and exercise our creative powers.

"Leverage strengths, manage weaknesses."

This seems simple – focus on and leverage your creative strengths. Remember don't try and do everything, weaknesses are mitigated through collaboration. After all, none of us are creative superheroes! Allowing others to share in the creative process will provide a conduit of constant and varied creative strengths. That's why an orchestra sounds so glorious playing together! The success of the whole is determined by the strength of the parts.

"Listen, think, add value."

Some of my best creative solutions and musical scores have come from listening to others. Whether it is the feedback from a director, a suggestion from my orchestrator, or considering a different dramatic approach to a scene from the film, *listening* and *thinking* have certainly added value to my creative self, as well as added value to the overall project.

These core principles of Panasonic, established by Matsushita back in the 1930's, continue to serve as its foundation today. "One can," as he often told people, "learn from any experience, and at any age." Konosuke Matsushita knew how to direct creativity by knowing the value of every employee, their experience and their own ability to assist in the innovation process.

Mastering these skills of *Directing Creativity* in yourself means you are now poised to step up to the podium, pick up the baton and conduct your own creativity!

CHAPTER 9

❖

CONDUCTING CREATIVITY

The Symphony

There is great power as I pick up the baton, raise my hands and signal the orchestra to begin playing. The simple act of giving a downbeat cue from the podium begins the musical motion. It triggers the commencement of sound by the orchestral machine of musicians.

The great American composer and conductor Leonard Bernstein loudly proclaimed, "I'm not interested in having an orchestra sound like itself. I want it to sound like the composer." Only the gifted conductors will mold and transform the sound of the orchestra. Only the skilled conductors will transform the musical performance by shaping the subtle nuance of interpretation into a truly moving experience for the audience. It is the conductor who is solely responsible for the cohesive and unique performance of the musical work. He or she alone determines the voice of the composer's notes.

Conducting creativity in others cannot begin until you are *Directing Creativity* in your own personal life. All creatives understand this and now that you are equipped to be a director of creativity, you are prepared to conduct it with others.

Inspire the dream in others to conduct creativity.

The great civil rights leader Martin Luther King knew how to inspire others. His mantra was, "I have a dream." Not, "I have a plan." He knew you must communicate your passion and love for the dream and let others share in the formulation of the plan.

Charles Dickens said, "The whole difference between construction and creation is exactly this; that a thing constructed can only be loved after it is constructed; but a thing created is loved before it exists."

The French writer, poet and pioneering aviator Antoine de Saint-Exupery said, "If you want to build a ship, don't herd people together to collect wood and don't assign them tasks and work, but rather teach them to long for the endless immensity of the sea."

One of the secrets in conducting creativity in others can be found in studies conducted on the development of creativity in children. It can be enhanced by certain components. In her book *Day Care and Early Education,* Alicia Pagano describes that these components include; an open environment, the active use of creative skills, the result of previous knowledge, a disciplined use of technique, and an association with artists.

Consider this, if the conditions of an open environment and creative liberties are essential for children's development, can you imagine how critical they are to inspire and conduct creativity in others? According to Steve Jobs, "You cannot mandate productivity. You must provide the tools to let people become their best."

While creating this climate for creativity, a little conducting will be required. This starts by *empowering* people with creative vision and giving them *permission* to direct their own creativity.

For me, I love working with directors who inspire my creativity. Those directors who encourage me to direct my own creativity within their broader view have always provided me with my most rewarding creative experiences.

There is however, a challenging practice today in Hollywood when "temporary" music is added into a cut of a film. Before I begin work composing the original score, this temporary music is added to aid the film's editor in determining the pace of the scenes. This "temp" music acts as a guide for the director, producer and studio execs to form their musical approach.

The challenge? The more a "temp track" is used, the more a composer is cut out of the "creative loop". No longer does a blank canvas exist, rather it's now a canvas cluttered with numerous other musical ideas. These ideas can be helpful, but more often than not they become problematic. The creative boundaries have already been established before a composer was able to share in this important step in the creative process.

I always welcome the blank page of possibility, the virgin canvas absent of music. Here I can utilize all of my imagination to fill the screen with a rich score.

When presented a film with a blank musical canvas, the film's director and producer have granted me permission to direct creativity. While they are ultimately the directors and control the final creative decisions, I have learned that at this point in the process that the smartest conductors of creativity know and exercise the value of unleashing creative freedom throughout the entire team.

"Listen to anyone with an original idea," said William McKnight, the president of 3M, "no matter how absurd it may sound at first. If you put fences around people, you get sheep. Give others the room they need."

As a conductor, I encourage the musicians to follow me while we navigate the score, but I don't dictate their every musical step. It is their personality and expertise that brings out the best in the music. I do conduct them, but only together do we all direct creativity.

My greatest recordings were always filled with individual passion from each singular musician channeled together, directed by the conductor, to achieve a musical masterpiece. I employed each of them to bring their point of view to the recording session, striving to get the best that is *within* them, not the best that I can project *on* them. I give them creative latitude within the boundaries provided on the written page of music. At times those parameters can be very narrow, while other times there is exciting flexibility.

Pick up the baton. You are the conductor *Directing Creativity* in others. Will you wield it with crushing control? Or will you be receptive to inspiring the interpretations of others?

In my experience, the final product or performance will far exceeded my own creativity as I invite, encourage and embrace creativity from others. George Kneller said, "It seems to be one of the paradoxes of creativity that in order to think originally, we must familiarize ourselves with the ideas of others."

Seek out input from others around you and drive innovation from the bottom up rather than dictating from the top down. To do this you must first learn to conduct this creativity from within.

Conducting creativity requires strong creative leadership.

Avul Pakir Jainulabdeen Abduo Kalam was a career scientist who studied physics and aerospace engineering. After four decades as a scientist and science administrator, he turned to politics. In 2002, he was elected the 11th President of India and was widely known as the "people's president."

Dr. Kalam refers to eight key tenets of creative leadership that are critical for driving innovation and growth. These are the eight tenets:

"The leader must have a vision for the organization."

That is exactly what conductors do. I can see *all* of the notes for the score, each musician, and every scene of the movie.

I have a clear end in mind before we begin recording the first note. My vision must be crystal clear first before the final score can be directed and captured.

> *"The leader must have the passion to transform that vision into action."*

My directors first instill this vision into me long before I begin composing. The best directors inspire me simply by telling me the story of the film, painting the mental image of the scenes and characters, and conveying the various emotions to me. It is literally passing the baton of creativity from director to composer. By communicating their vision and transferring that creative energy to me, my job is to not drop the baton but to keep the directors vision alive. I then transfer this creative vision to my musical team.

> *"The leader must be able to travel into the unexplored path."*

For a film's director, working with a composer is certainly an unexplored path. It is the step in filmmaking that is most frightful for many directors because music is often a language unfamiliar to them. They can express drama and emotion. Translating that into musical terms is nearly impossible for them. Great directors trust their composers and are willing to venture into those uncharted waters of uncertainty to discover the greatest musical solutions that breathes life into their film.

"The leader must know how to manage both success and failure."

As mentioned before, not every creative idea will be brilliant. In fact, most will not be. Knowing that failure will also accompany success removes the trepidation. When failure occurs, creativity will provide another solution by restarting the innovation process. Strive for those better results – they are there to be discovered.

"The leader must have the courage to make decisions."

You are the one standing at the podium. You are the one holding the baton. The "orchestra" is looking to you for encouragement, determination and direction. They are looking to you for leadership. Boldly take the baton, and lead them with confidence.

"The leader should have nobility in management."

Pointing out success in others may be one of the noblest acts of leadership. The confidence of the orchestra grows as I acknowledge and praise the musician who performs well. From the podium, I alone influence and affect the atmosphere or 'vibe' of all recording sessions. A confidence, along with careful correction, signals to the group that you are a seasoned conductor – a great leader.

"Every action of the leader should be transparent."

Success and failure of the team are shared together with the conductor. While it's easy to celebrate only the wins, I have learned that as a leader acknowledging mistakes actually elicits more cooperation from the group. The orchestra is always pulling for me to succeed and when I am honest with myself and with them, they will rally around me as their conductor – their leader.

"The leader must work with integrity and succeed with integrity."

All leaders and conductors know this. I am not superior to anyone else in the orchestra. As the conductor, I too am part of the orchestra. We are all assembled together with the same goal in mind; realizing the best film score possible. Great conductors do this with integrity.

Dr. Kalam shared that he once encountered a leader with all the qualities of the eight tenants. It was when India's first satellite launch mission failed in 1979, the chairman of the Indian space agency Professor Satish Dhawan took full responsibility for the failure, even though Dr. Kalam was actually the mission director.

The following year, when they successfully placed the first Indian-built satellite in orbit, Professor Dhawan didn't attend the press conference. Instead he asked Dr. Kalam to share the success story with the media, giving Dr. Kalam full credit for the mission's success.

Like Professor Dhawan and Dr. Kalam, I am fully aware that it is also impossible for me to succeed in *Directing Creativity* alone. My creativity, sparked by those who struggled through pre-production and production of the movie, only grows stronger as I begin composing the score. It is the combined efforts of the team that results in the final movie score. Yes I conduct it, but everyone shared in the creative process, and I make it a point to celebrate the collaboration of everyone attached to the production of a film.

Questions are the catalyst for creativity.

Questions invite and ignite opportunities. All questions are valid, even the perceived "dumb questions."

Picasso asked a perceived dumb question, "Is it possible to depict the human form in some other way?" His question led to the birth of cubism. Steve Jobs asked lots of presumed dumb questions. "Should a cell phone do more than make phone calls?" As of 2017 Apple has sold more than one billion iphones worldwide. It's safe to say that was not really a dumb question at all. Instead, it was a question that propelled Apple into becoming one of the greatest companies ever.

Remember:

- Creativity always begins with a question.

- The quality of the question determines the quality of creativity.

- Frame your questions while considering an approach to the circumstances, problems, needs and opportunities.

- Rather than asking "how" questions, focus on questions that will illicit creative responses and solutions.

- "What would happen if ..." questions opens up new and exciting creative considerations.

I continue to learn the art of questions, as they:

- Provide creative leverage for me as I'm creating.

- Offer me direction and call my attention to hidden details.

- Open my eyes, my ears and indeed my entire creative being to possibilities I have never considered.

- Solve problems, invite participation from others and are vital to *Directing Creativity*.

You will discover the hidden secrets by asking questions. Keep in mind that the creative director's vision for the final outcome does not need to be complete at the outset, in fact it should not be. So go ahead and question everything, from every angle, and super fuel your creativity!

This questioning may also require a general herding of ideas. Some are specific like, "Go left now". Others may coax a general direction, "Tend toward the left." To get the most out of your creative direction ask questions like, "What if you look over there?" Asking yourself and your team "What if" questions will challenge your most pre-determined courses, offering the greatest reward.

Create a playing field of unlimited possibilities.

Questions require a balance of "restricting" and "letting emerge." Offering a vision via questions means directing creativity to the fullest, while providing enough open space to capture an emerging concept or idea. The constraints should be tight enough to constitute a strong challenge. They should be restrictive in some form, while now inviting and igniting creativity from within those boundaries.

Piers Ibbotson and Lotte Darse wrote about such an example as they shared how 'good constraints' helped in the development of the Sony Walkman. The story goes that the CEO went down to the research labs where all of the techs and engineers were working. He gathered them round and pulled out of his shirt pocket a small block of wood. He held it up and said, "Make me a tape-player this big", put it down on the table and left.

Why was the block of wood such a good constraint? It was specific. The team members could pick it up and start measuring it. They could respond immediately to the challenge that focused them in the right direction. If effect, this is really a good constraint because of what was NOT said. The CEO didn't say:

- "Make me the smallest tape recorder you can." (They'd probably still be at it.)

- "Make me a small portable tape player." (They might have come up with something too big to fit in your shirt pocket.)

- "Make something new and revolutionary that will let people play music wherever they want" (No point in encouraging them to re-invent the wheel.)

Instead, he met with the team in person, gave a controlled performance in front of the people who would be doing the work, and left them to it, leaving plenty of space for them to imagine, invent and innovate, but within concrete and specific boundaries that he had personally communicated.

The CEO had a partial vision of the desired outcome, but with no idea of how it could be done. Therefore, rather than giving his team a target to hit, he basically gave them a field to play in.

When creating this playing field of unlimited possibilities, provide just enough rules, regulations and constraints. Then get out of the way. You have assembled the team already, so give them creative freedom within the rules of the game. Let them play, let them discover, let them create.

Boundaries and constraints can provide a conduit of creativity.

When I wrote the score to *Cowgirls n' Angels* for 20th Century Fox Studios, the budgetary constraints allowed me to only have a small ensemble of musicians to record the score. My first instincts were to compose a score much larger in scope. The genre seemed to warrant such a score but the music budget did not allow it. I was at a creative crossroad; I could write a score from my sample libraries emulating a large orchestra, or I could search for another creative approach.

The film seemed to need a large sound, or so I thought. It wasn't until I began trying out simple melodies for solo instruments that I discovered a greater emotional connection with the characters. James Cromwell's character seemed deeper, more believable and stronger when accompanied only by a solo guitar. Bailee Madison's character appeared more innocent and vulnerable when only a piano underscored her performances.

These budgetary boundaries focused my creative choices in non-traditional directions. They made me look deeper into the characters and search for solutions, while staying true to the story being told.

Yes, a large orchestra would have worked. In fact it would have been the easier path to create such a score. But the small, intimate approach of scoring *Cowgirls n' Angels* with only guitar, woodwinds and piano provided the audience with an honest depiction of each of the characters. The simple, solo instruments of the score directed the audience to look closer at what each character said and how the other characters responded to their dialogue. This musical approach signaled the viewer to look deeper into each scene of the film and focused the drama more on the characters. The music provided the emotional connection not only between the characters, but gave the audience a personal stake in the story and a connection to each character. In short, the simple approach of the score provided for a more poignant story to unfold.

My experience has demonstrated that the best directors tend to offer limited direction. They set the parameters, balance their direction with silence, and then observe my creative process. They look for the music fragments to latch onto and then use them for their future creative direction. They coax, nudge and encourage me, within the parameters, to direct my own creativity. They are master conductors.

Master conductors effectively:

- Stimulate and encourage curiosity and exploration.

- Inspire confidence and a willingness to take risks.

- Provide opportunities for choice and discovery.

- Solve problems that do not have well-defined answers.

- Find, recognize and reward creativity.

- Create an environment where tradition can be challenged.

I love working with these master conductors of creativity. They always seem to get the most out of my creative potential. They understand conducting creativity means collaborating, encouraging and exhibiting patience for brilliant ideas to arrive.

Great conductors have discovered that these are the secrets to masterful performances, while seasoned conductors strive for excellence in each of these areas. The greatest conductors of creativity know every note and nuance and they skillfully lead their group to creating a masterpiece. So take the baton with confidence. Lead your symphony, as you conduct creativity.

CHAPTER 10

❖

THAT'S A WRAP!

The Art of Innovation

I t was a morning in 852 AD in the city of Cordoba, Spain. Astronomer, glassworker, musician, engineer, thinker and inventor Abbas Ibn Firnas literally leaped his way into history.

Ibn Firnas sported a cloak resembling huge wings made out of a coat reinforced with wooden pieces that acted as type of glider. He saw this coat as his "wings".

He climbed onto the minaret of Cordoba's largest Masjid and jumped off. While this parachute-like coat was not enough to break his fall completely, it apparently managed to slow him down sufficiently to sustain only minor injuries. Even though he failed in this attempt to fly, he used the innovation process perfectly.

For years, he joined the ancient Greeks and Egyptians in the desire to be the first to build a machine that would allow flight. First Ibn Firnas imagined what it would be like to fly free as a bird and glide through the air.

Imagine, **makes a way for the** *inception* **of creativity.**

It was however, his first failed attempt at flight that initiated Ibn Firnas to truly apply a proper sequencing of the innovation process. For the next 23 years, Ibn Firnas studied birds, falling seeds, leaves, feathers and even bats.

Incubate **ideas, wait for greater** *insight.*

Ibn Firnas devoted many of those years to building the first modern glider with wings of silk, wood and actual feathers.

Improvise, **uncovering clear** *intention.*

After literally falling once, Ibn Firnas was determined to fly rather than fail. He worked through the innovation process over and over to make the necessary improvements to his flying machine.

Integrate and *Inspect,* providing *illumination* for *improvements.*

Finally in 875, Ibn Firnas was ready again to test his life-long dream of flying. The spectacle was not without its fair share of critics. One on-looker wrote, "We thought Ibn Firnas certainly mad and we feared for his life!" Abbas Ibn Firnas would not be dissuaded. He was convinced his creativity would take flight.

One afternoon in 875, a few people gathered on a hill in Spain to witness the 65 year-old Ibn Firnas' attempt to fly. He arrived in a suit of feathers, with actual wings of two large birds attached to his arms and legs. After being assisted to the top of a wall on the hill, he confidently addressed the spectators below, "Presently I shall take leave of you. By guiding these wings up and down, I should ascend like the birds. If all goes well, after soaring for a time I should be able to return safely to your side."

When a favoring wind appeared, Ibn Firnas launched himself from atop the hill into the air. He manipulated the two sets of wings in the movements he had worked out on paper. He flailed his way to an altitude higher than the point from which he had taken off. Gliding through the air for several hundred feet, he turned and soared back remaining airborne for a full 10 minutes over the fertile plains outside of Cordoba.

"He flew faster than the phoenix in his flight when he dressed his body in the feathers of a vulture," exclaimed one onlooker. "He flew a considerable distance as if he had been a bird," recorded another witness.

Only upon landing did he realize that he had omitted a critical part of his design, he needed something like a bird's tail that allowed for a controlled descent. This realization came too late. Ibn Firnas hit the ground fast and hard injuring his back and leaving him in pain for the rest of his life.

1,000 years before Orville and Wilbur Wright took flight at Kittyhawk and 700 years before da Vinci's famous fly machine sketches, it was Abbas Ibn Firnas who vaulted from the safety of the earth to fly and soar like a bird. It was Ibn Firnas who succeeded, as he invented a flying machine and become the first to ever fly!

The art of innovation was fully realized by Abbas Ibn Firnas. Beautiful, artful, graceful, challenging, innovative, daring and creative all describe his passion to fly. His dream was fully executed through the application of the steps in this process of innovation.

"The mind can proceed only so far upon what it knows and can prove. There comes a point where the mind takes a higher plane of knowledge, but can never prove how it got there. All great discoveries have involved such a leap." Although Albert Einstein described a figurative leap, it was Ibn Firnas who literally took that leap and changed history forever.

"Around here, we don't look backwards for very long. We keep moving forward, opening up new doors and doing new things, because we're curious and curiosity keeps leading us down new paths." Although Walt Disney said this, any great innovator knows it to be true. It is this curiosity that leads to igniting the imagination.

The art of innovation requires a curious attitude.

Following the aviation dream of Ibn Firnas, the French writer of *The Little Prince* and pioneering aviator Antoine Saint-Exupery professed, "A pile of rocks ceases to be a rock pile when somebody contemplates it with the idea of a cathedral in mind."

It is the rock pile of possibility and curiosity that gives way to the art of innovation. It is creativity that constructs the castles for kings.

Consider the innovation process as a well-marked road map with clear sign posts along the way, guiding us to a desired destination of innovation:

> *Imagination* begins the journey leading to *inception*. *Incubation* is the rest stop along the way, providing the necessary step, refueling our creativity, yielding *insight*. *Improvising*, sketching or brainstorming allows consideration of how to bring into reality the *Imagination*. This step leads to *intention*. Through the collaboration or *Integration* with others, we arrive at the moment of *illumination*, that light-bulb moment of discovery. Now we arrive at the point of *Inspection*, striving for *improvement*. Finally, we reach our destination, *inventing* our dream, creating our imagination – *Innovation*.

This innovation process provides clarity along the path of creation. At no point along the way can we move on to the next step until we have reached the outcome of the current step. Only then when the outcome is manifest, can we move on to the next step. Similarly, when we reach an obstacle along the way, returning to a previous step in the process will provide an opportunity to try again at the particular step and gain a clearer outcome.

The innovation process is not a destination. It is a journey!

The innovation process repeats itself over and over. It's circular in nature. It propels us to look deeper at creation. Just like a wheel, it turns over and over, returning to the beginning in order for motion to continue. Each step along the path requires application of the innovation process. Each hurdle and challenge can be solved and overcome by applying the five steps.

Armed with the five steps of the innovation process, you know how to direct creativity! You know the process. You are prepared for each step of illumination along the path of discovery.

Each time you direct your creativity, you sharpen your skills of innovation. Don't get discouraged if your first few attempts at directing creativity do not yield groundbreaking achievements. With each attempt, you strengthen your creative potential. You train yourself to follow the process.

Noted Stanford professor Elliot Eisner said that there are four types of creative people:

1. Aesthetic Organizers – those who reorganize preexisting ideas and concepts.

2. Boundary Pushers – those who take an existing idea and push it a little further.

3. Inventors – those who take existing knowledge and create new ideas.

4. Boundary Breakers *(the rarest group)* – the Leonardos and Copernicuses.

You need not wait to discover that you are the next Leonardo da Vinci. Nor should you get discouraged if you do not appear to be a "boundary breaker." Take advantage of your creativity where you are. Start simple and small and cultivate your creativity. *Begin by beginning!*

Don't wait for creativity to find you. Go out and meet it!

As you view the future, things will continue to go on as they are currently or they might change due to some marvelous invention. Consider this future as a result of *your* plans and *your* creativity.

"Twenty years from now," said Mark Twain, "you will be more disappointed by the things that you didn't do than by the ones you did do. So throw off the bowlines. Sail away from the safe harbor. Catch the trade winds in your sails. Explore. Dream. Discover."

Imagine, Incubate, Improvise, Integrate and *Inspect* are your steps to innovate. This 5-step Innovation Process guides you. So go be creative!

**Learn to direct your creativity and
You can predict the future by inventing it!**

This is *THE ART OF INNOVATION.*

***

ABOUT THE AUTHOR

A lan Williams is a multiple award-winning Hollywood film and television composer of more than 100 films, including the Academy Award nominated IMAX film *Amazon*. Randall Larson from *Soundtrack Magazine* wrote, *"Alan Williams film and television scores provide a fluidity of melody and enough varied nuances of texture and style to make his work defy categorization."*

As a speaker, Alan has traveled the world teaching creativity and innovation before world leaders and business titans in more than 30 countries. He continues to reach wide global audiences through his TEDx talk *"Creativity: The Power to Trend"* along with his highly engaging seminars, training and keynotes from his consulting firm, Silverscreen Consulting.

CONTACT ALAN

To get the latest updates visit:

www.alanwilliams.com

Alan speaks frequently on the topic of Creativity and Innovation. He can deliver a keynote, half-day, full day or multi-day workshops and seminars. If you are interested to find out more, please visit:

www.silverscreenconsulting.com

You may also connect with Alan here:

Twitter: twitter.com/moviecomposer

Facebook: facebook.com/Silverscreen-Consulting

$\mathcal{S}$ilverscreen Consulting
Innovative Solutions

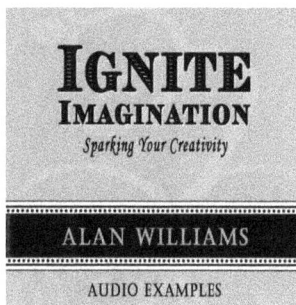

Creativity simply is the mental process of generating new ideas or concepts. Any idea, process or product is a result of creativity. IGNITE IMAGINATION: SPARKING YOUR CREATIVITY is designed to spark the creative process. As you practice and apply the principles in this book, you will unlock the power of your imagination, light the flame of creativity and unleash your creative potential.

Get the companion audio download album, IGNITE IMAGINATION: AUDIO EXAMPLES for all of the interactive audio exercises.

Discover at www.silverscreenconsulting.com

Silverscreen Consulting
Innovative Solutions

21 Brainstorming Techniques That Work

Alan Williams

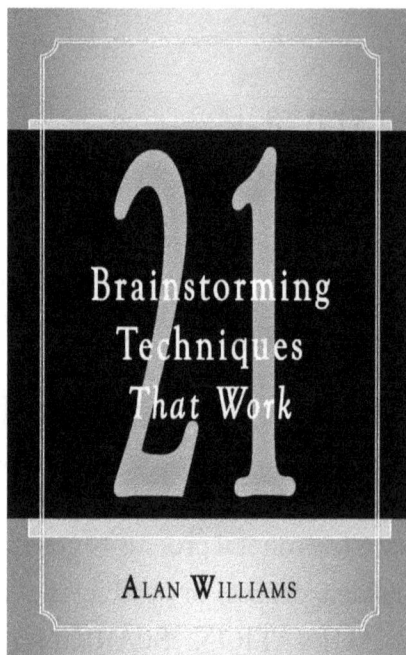

Brainstorming is the act of stimulating creative thinking and developing new ideas. 21 BRAINSTORMING TECHNIQUES THAT WORK will provide direction, focus and the process to creative solutions. These techniques offer a variety of approaches for individuals, small groups and even large group settings. Get ready to discover solutions!

Discover at www.silverscreenconsulting.com

Silverscreen Consulting
Innovative Solutions

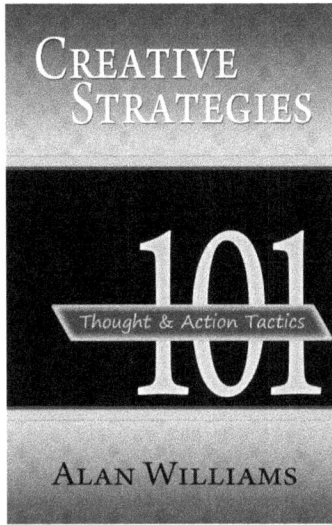

101 CREATIVE STRATEGIES are a set of 52 cards with *thought* and *action* tactics to creatively aid your discovery of solutions. Begin with thought tactics to consider focus, direction and strategy. Some action tactics will manifest themselves directly as a result of the thought tactics. Other actions will be determined from action tactics themselves. The sequence of the CREATIVE STRATEGIES is not important. Pick any of the 101 tactics and begin. Strategize to maximize your outcome. Change your tactics and you will change your results!

Discover at www.silverscreenconsulting.com

$\int$ ilverscreen Consulting
Innovative Solutions

www.ingramcontent.com/pod-product-compliance
Lightning Source LLC
Chambersburg PA
CBHW070716220326
41598CB00024BA/3184